HighTide

Plays: 1

Ditch

peddling

The Big Meal

Lampedusa

Ditch: 'Steel's text is an evocative mix of farm metaphors, punchy dialogue and moments of dreamy wistfulness.' *Tribune*

peddling: 'Feels like the intersection of Beckett and Albee.' *New York Times, Critics' Choice*

The Big Meal: 'A life-in-overdrive comic drama . . . Dan LeFranc's snappy dialogue captures the tumultuous tenor of family gatherings.' *New York Times*

Lampedusa: 'One of the most gently enticing pieces of storytelling you will see, softly encroaching on the moral consciousness like a lullaby. . . . Lustgarten's descriptions of drowning have a power that comes from fleshy detail matched by poetic virtuosity.' *The Times*

T0353276

HighTide
Plays: 1

Ditch
peddling
The Big Meal
Lampedusa

with an introduction by Steven Atkinson,
Artistic Director of HighTide

Bloomsbury Methuen Drama
An imprint of Bloomsbury Publishing Plc

B L O O M S B U R Y
LONDON · OXFORD · NEW YORK · NEW DELHI · SYDNEY

Bloomsbury Methuen Drama

An imprint of Bloomsbury Publishing Plc

Imprint previously known as Methuen Drama

50 Bedford Square	1385 Broadway
London	New York
WC1B 3DP	NY 10018
UK	USA

www.bloomsbury.com

BLOOMSBURY, METHUEN DRAMA and the Diana logo are trademarks of Bloomsbury Publishing Plc

Ditch first published in 2010 by Methuen Drama © 2010, 2016

This version of the script features some changes to the script

peddling first published in 2014 by Methuen Drama and in 2015 with changes to the script © 2014, 2015, 2016

The Big Meal first published in 2013 by Methuen Drama in *The Methuen Drama Book of New American Plays* © 2013, 2016

Lampedusa first published in 2015 by Methuen Drama © 2015, 2016

This version of the script features some changes to the script

Introduction first published in this collection © Steven Atkinson 2016

British Library Cataloguing-in-Publication Data
A catalogue record for this book is available from the British Library.

ISBN: PB: 978-1-3500-0196-1
ePDF: 978-1-3500-0197-8
ePub: 978-1-3500-0198-5

Library of Congress Cataloging-in-Publication Data
A catalog record for this book is available from the Library of Congress.

Cover design: Olivia D'Cruz
Cover image © Getty Images/stevendocwra

Typeset by Mark Heslington Ltd, Scarborough, North Yorkshire

Contents

HighTide
Select Chronology

2007   HighTide is formed as a new theatre company in
        Suffolk, England. The first HighTide Festival is held in
        Halesworth in March with short plays by Tom Basden,
        Steven Bloomer, Sarah Cuddon, Sam Holcroft, Matthew
        Morrison, Pericles Snowdon, Megan Walsh and Iain
        Weatherby

2008   The HighTide Festival is held in May. Premieres include:
        Switzerland by Nick Payne; *Certain Dark Things* by Emily
        Watson Howes; *I Caught Crabs in Walberswick* by Joel
        Horwood (and transfer to the Bush Theatre); *Stovepipe* by
        Adam Brace (and transfer to London with the National
        Theatre and Bush Theatre)

2009   Festival programme includes: *Muhmah* by Jesse Weaver;
        Guardians by Lucy Caldwell; *Fixer* by Lydia Adetunji; *One
        Evening* by Schubert Winterreise, translated by Michael
        Symmons Roberts and Samuel Beckett (co-production
        with Aldeburgh Music); *Berlin/Wall* by David Hare (co-
        production with Aldeburgh Music);

2010   Festival includes the premieres of *Lidless* by Frances Ya-
        Chu Cowhig (and transfer to Trafalgar Studios); *Ditch* by
        Beth Steel (and transfer to the Old Vic Tunnels); *Moscow
        Lives* by Serge Cartwright; *Famine Diary* by Jesse Weaver

2011   Festival programme includes: *Nicked* book and lyrics by
        Richard Marsh, music by Natalia Sheppard; *Dusk Rings
        a Bell* by Stephen Belber (and transfer to Watford Palace
        Theatre); *Midnight Your Time* by Adam Brace; *Incoming* by
        Andrew Motion

2012   HighTide Festival expands programme and includes
        premieres of *Clockwork* by Laura Poliakoff; *Boys* by Ella
        Hickson (and transfer to Nuffield Theatre and Soho
        Theatre); *Seizing Cinderella* by Stephanie Street; *The
        Adventure* by Oliver Birch; *The Best Years of Your Life*; *Binary*
        by Alexandra Wood and Ian McHugh; *Brunch Plays*
        by various; *The Agony and Ecstasy of Steve Jobs* by Mike
        Daisy; *Bethany* by Laura Marks (co-production with the
        Public Theatre New York); *The Hour of Feeling* by Mona
        Mansour (co-production with the Public Theatre New
        York); *Neighbors* by Branden Jacob-Jenkins (co-production

with the Public Theatre New York); *Perish* by Stella Fawn
Ragsdale (co-production with the Public Theatre New
York); *Organs of Little Apparent Importance* by Jon McLeod;
Eisteddfod by Luke Barnes; *Educating Ronnie* by Joe
Douglas; *Mudlarks* by Vickie Donoghue (and transfer to
Theatre503 and the Bush Theatre)

2013   Festival programme includes the premieres of *Pastoral*
by Thomas Eccleshare (and transfer to Soho Theatre);
Smallholding by Chris Dunkley (and transfer to Nuffield
Theatre and Soho Theatre); *Moth* by Declan Greene (and
transfer to the Bush Theatre); *Neighbors* by Branden
Jacobs-Jenkins (and transfer to Nuffield Theatre). Outside
the festival HighTide produced *Stuart: A Life Backwards*
by Jack Thorne (Sheffield Theatres and Watford Palace
Theatre)

2014   Festival programme includes: *The Big Meal* by Dan
LeFranc (and transfer to the Ustinov Theatre, Bath);
peddling by Harry Melling (and transfer to 59E59 New
York City and the Arcola Theatre); *Incognito* by Nick
Payne (and transfer to Live Theatre Newcastle and the
Bush Theatre); *The Girl's Guide to Saving the World* by
Elinor Cook

2015   Festival changes location to Aldeburgh, Suffolk and
is held in September. Programme includes: *Harrogate*
by Al Smith; *BRENDA* by E V Crowe (and transfer to
the Yard Theatre); *So Here We Are* by Luke Norris (and
transfer to the Royal Exchange Theatre); *Lampedusa* by
Anders Lustgarten (and transfer to Soho Theatre and
Unity Theatre Liverpool). Outside the festival HighTide
produced *Forget Me Not* by Tom Holloway (Bush Theatre)

2016   Festival programme includes: *The Sugar-Coated Bullets of
the Bourgeoisie* by Anders Lustgarten (and transfer to the
Arcola Theatre); *Girls* by Theresa Ikoko (and transfer
to Birmingham Repertory Theatre and Soho Theatre);
Pilgrims by Elinor Cook (and transfer to the Yard Theatre
and Theatr Clwyd); *In Fidelity* by Rob Drummond (and
transfer to the Traverse Theatre). *The Path*, a tenth-
anniversary production written by HighTide alumni,
premieres on 10 September 2016. Outside the festival
HighTide produced *Harrogate* by Al Smith (Royal Court
Theatre and tour) and *The Brolly Project* (Young Vic)

A Decade of Influencing the Mainstream:
An Introduction

In 2009, a play called *2050* arrived in our offices opposite Smithfield meat market. Who is this Beth Steel? As I read it I met a mind bracing against the physical and conceptual boundaries of theatre. With its gallows humour and primal imagery, the meat market connection was not incidental.

A partnership between the 1,000-seat Old Vic theatre in London's Waterloo, and our tiny new plays company was an unlikely one. But nevertheless I was told that its Artistic Director, Kevin Spacey, wanted to see me. We met backstage after a performance of *Inherit the Wind*, with Kevin in as much stage make-up as Sir from Ronald Harwood's *The Dresser*. As we talked he held his dog underarm, and as a dog owner myself we hit it off. The notion of co-producing Beth's play, now called *Ditch*, was a done deal.

Ditch opened the fantastically unlikely Old Vic Tunnels, which for three years was the Old Vic's second space, situated underneath Waterloo Station. It hosted everything from emerging artists to Bill Clinton. In the main house was Sam Mendes's *As You Like It* and *The Tempest*. The Old Vic team were game selling Shakespeare and Steel side-by-side. The Tunnels were, of course, quixotic. I remember all too well the challenges of guiding audiences from The Vic down Station Approach. The Tunnels were ice cold even in July. But it was a triumph of will for Spacey who to this day remains committed to making opportunities for new talent.

Ditch had a tepid critical response, and open hostility from the *Evening Standard*. I remember the morning the Sundays came out, and the juxtaposition of walking on a sunny morning through Ladbroke Grove whilst listening to Beth's heart breaking on the phone. 'They're killing me.' Thankfully talent won out. In 2014 Beth's second play, *Wonderland*, opened to wide acclaim at Hampstead Theatre.

And in a brilliant twist, Beth won the Evening Standard Award for Most Promising Playwright. As I write this her third play, *Labyrinth*, is set to open this autumn, again at Hampstead. Set in context, the three plays now illustrate a talent capable of writing on a big canvas, worldly, funny and character-driven dramas.

As a post note, nobody in Halesworth, where HighTide Festival 2009 took place, believed that the man in the red baseball cap, flanked by two assistants, was Kevin Spacey. We had dinner in the only restaurant serving past 9 pm, and as word got out the adjoining pub started to fill with locals. The entire population of Halesworth could fit in the Old Vic's auditorium in one sitting. We exited into the pub and Spacey the showman emerged, warm and gracious to the stunned onlookers. Whether or not it was actually Spacey remains today a hotly contested myth in the town to those who weren't there that night.

***

Our offices in Smithfield Market are provided in kind through the extraordinary generosity of Lansons. In our rehearsal studio there I first saw Harry Melling give a scratch performance of his play *peddling*. The audience of fifty were electrified, both by this humane and distinctive poetic script, and by Harry's totally compelling delivery of it.

Harry, the designer Lily Arnold and I eventually settled on the idea to stage *peddling* in a gauze cube. Thus the audience could see Harry, but Harry could not see them. To date HighTide has staged over fifty productions, and one of the most astonishing images for me remains the moment when the gauze dropped. After sixty minutes of solo performance, Harry sat naked, exhausted, looking directly at his audience for the first time. Smiling.

Following the opening at HighTide Festival 2014, the production team all flew straight to New York to open Off-Broadway. The American producers perhaps understandably made a big deal out of Harry's Harry Potter connection. At the same time as we were there, Daniel Radcliffe was performing on Broadway in *The Lieutenant of Inishmore*. Walking down 10th Avenue one day, Harry, whilst being grateful to the films, pondered if he would ever shake Potter. Watching him in *peddling* there was no trace of Dudley Dursley.

The idea for *peddling* originated in Harry as a young child opening the front door of his London house to a pedlar. His mum turned the salesman away. The boy went crazy, throwing stones at Harry's windows. When we transferred to the Arcola in London, during one performance there was a commotion in the audience. In the sold out house, filled largely with young audiences, an argument had broken out between a man and a young girl on her phone. He wasn't to know that that night we'd worked with the sadly now defunct Kids Company to bring disadvantaged young Londoners to the show. This girl, it transpired, was going through turmoil with her boyfriend and couldn't block it out. Ashamed, she wrote an apology letter to Harry. The apology recounted every narrative beat of the play, less to prove that she was paying attention, but instead demonstrating why this was the best play that she had ever seen. For Harry his journey had come full circle.

***

I first met Laurence Boswell in 2013 in a cafe on Old Compton Street. He was both a West End director of repute, and now led the Ustinov Studio in Bath, which was giving fantastically well received premieres to new plays. I wanted HighTide to co-produce with Bath and I steeled myself to make this case. I hardly spoke in this ninety-minute meeting. Instead I heard an extraordinary cautionary tale about Laurence's rise and perceived fall, which apexed on his being over-stretched and failing to deliver in his theatre productions and films. As I was then, a 28-year-old director, his story was both terrifying and illuminating. It served as a reminder to walk rather than run.

I was unsuccessful pitching Robert Icke to him as director. But we did, however, agree on a play. In the UK there was a growing awareness that we had a very good generation of emerging playwrights. Talents that HighTide had produced such as Jack Thorne, Ella Hickson, Nick Payne and Sam Holcroft. And this trend was being mirrored in America with Brandon Jacobs Jenkins, Frances Ya-Chu Cowhig and Annie Baker. Dan LeFranc is a peer of the aforementioned, and his beautifully observed play *The Big Meal* told a universal story about family via an elegant and devastating structural conceit. This was challenging for Bath. In fact it would be challenging for any theatre: an unknown young writer to UK audiences and a relatively large cast.

Reassurance came in an unexpected form. Michael Boyd led the Royal Shakespeare Company for a decade. Under his leadership the company got its mojo back as he created a broad church for traditionalists and radicals like Rupert Goold and Filter, and commissioned new work including the mega-hit *Matilda*. I was as surprised as anyone that Michael's first show after leaving the RSC would be for HighTide. He said that he'd heard the younger directors in the RSC talk about the company and 'it sounded cool.' Michael's participation in the HighTide Festival caught the imagination of audiences in Suffolk and today we continue to benefit from an expanding audience.

***

As I write this introduction, the refugee crisis in Europe from North Africa is ongoing. As of 2016, over 60 million people across the planet are currently displaced from their homes – more than at any time in history.

I was nervous to meet Anders Lustgarten. In his final season at the helm of the Royal Court, Dominic Cooke produced Anders's play *If You Don't Let Us Dream, We Won't Let You Sleep*.

When promoting it, Anders had caused a few ripples in the press, especially in a provocative interview with the *Evening Standard*, accompanied by a picture of Anders screaming and putting two fingers up. I discovered that Anders is not a retiring person. As we had coffee in Holborn he spoke with the fevered passion of a conspiracy theorist: 'This shit *is* happening in the Med, the c**ts just aren't reporting it.' As we started rehearsals for *Lampedusa* in March 2015, the refugee crisis, then referred to as the migrant crisis, started to headline the TV news. We'd come to rehearsals, our heads filled with what we read in the papers and watched on the news that morning.

Following its initial run in the Soho Theatre studio, we returned to play the main house that summer. There had been some consternation that the refugee crisis could be old news by then. In September when we were again in rehearsals for the HighTide Festival run, public opinion finally shifted away from the growing fear and xenophobia. Alan Kurdi, a three-year-old Syrian boy, washed up ashore in Bodrum, Turkey. His limp body lay flat, face down in the sand. At HighTide Festival 2015, we performed in a temporary venue on the Aldeburgh beach. On the opening night, with the wind rushing the dome and the sound of the sea outside, one audience member stood up mid-show and promptly fainted. The designer, Lucy Osborne and I staged *Lampedusa* in a wooden amphitheatre, with the audience sat on benches corkscrewing upwards, and the cast sat amongst them. Some audiences cried. Some were motivated to action. Others were affronted by Anders's mode of direct politics. Anders is admirably uncynical. His characters are testament to his belief that inherent in people is the capacity for good. It's an unfashionable way to write plays in a culture where extremes and sensationalism are valued. But he caught a moment with *Lampedusa*, and personalized an overwhelming global event where fear clouded ethics and empathy.

***

It was a rather invidious job that the editors of Methuen Drama and I had to select the plays in this volume. It is useful to note what the parameters were: first, to choose from the plays that have been published by Methuen Drama rather than other publishers. And second, we chose the plays that best illustrated the remarkable first ten years of HighTide. My colleagues and I have recently launched HighTide's tenth anniversary season. This year sees our annual festival now firmly established in Aldeburgh, and our productions playing in the Royal Court, Traverse, Soho, the Yard, Theatr Clwyd, the Arcola, Birmingham Rep and the Young Vic. We're lucky to have launched in a period of great new writers, and fortunate that many have chosen to entrust their plays to us.

HighTide's success is down to the writers, and the now thousands of directors, designers, actors, producers, advisors and funders who have clubbed behind this company in its mission to produce new artists. It's been my privilege to have worked with so many brilliant people. And I look forward to discovering all the new talent championed through HighTide in the years to come.

STEVEN ATKINSON

Amsterdam, June 2016

Steven is the Artistic Director and co-founder of HighTide.

Ditch

Beth Steel

For Mum and Dad

Ditch was first performed at the HighTide Festival on 30 April 2010 before transferring to the Old Vic Tunnels, London, on 13 May 2010 in a HighTide and Old Vic Theatre co-production. It featured the following cast and creative team:

James	Gethin Anthony
Turner	Sam Hazeldine
Megan	Matti Houghton
Mrs Peel	Dearbhla Molloy
Bug	Paul Rattray
Burns	Danny Webb
Director	Richard Twyman
Designer	Takis
Sound designer	Christopher Shutt
Lighting designer	Matt Prentice
Composer	Tom Mills

Setting

The Peak District. The future.

Characters

Both the women and men appear older than their given ages, due to labour in harsh weather and lost years.

Mrs Peel, *fifty-eight years old.*

Megan, *twenty years old.*

Burns, *early fifties.*

Bug, *late thirties.*

Turner, *late thirties.*

James, *twenty years old.*

Production note

The entire stage is to be covered thickly in barren peat. The peat should rise around the perimeter of the stage to create a shallow ditch where the action takes place. The peat is there to be interacted with, which is to say, as the characters rise and fall they will be covered in dirt.

Act One

Scene One

A remote farm, now a Security outpost in the Peak District. Plot of land. Early evening, the light is fading fast. The guttural croak of a raven overhead. Dogs bark.

Turner (*Off stage.*)   Woo-Hoo!

Turner *runs out followed by* **James**.

Turner (*Hollers out.*)   You jammy cunt! He's gonna be gloatin' all night.

James   Where's he takin' her?

Turner   Putting her in that outbuildin' over there. I been one ahead, now she makes us even.

James   You keep a score?

Turner   Ain't as if it's every day yer gettin' one. That's the first Illegal we picked up in six weeks.

James   What a' you doin' the rest a' the time?

Turner   Tuggin' our dicks. Out lookin' for the next ones s'what we doin'.

Turner *takes out his flask, belts back a drink.*

Most a' the time me and Bug over there a' out patrollin' together. But I'll have you with me for a few days, train you up and then you can go out with Burns.

James   Been given a letter for him.

Turner   Letter? How'd you get it?

James   Headquarters in Manchester.

Turner   You got it with yer now?

James *nods.*

Turner   Let me have a look at it.

James   It's sealed.

Turner   Ain't gonna open it.

James   S'what you want it for?

Turner   Just give me the fuckin' letter.

James *produces the letter.* **Turner** *snatches looks at the envelope.*

Turner   Shit.

James   What?

Turner   Can't tell what's in it.

Turner *gives the envelope to* **James**.

Turner   Burns's boy, Brian, been deployed three year ago.

James   Thinkin' he dead?

Turner   Probably says he comin' back, now that we got the stronghold over there.

Bug *enters jauntily.*

Bug   What'd you say to that then?

Turner   Yeah, alright. This here is big useless Greg.

James *and* **Bug** *shake hands.*

Bug   Bug.

James   James.

Bug   A we glad to see you.

James   Glad to be here.

Bug   They gettin' younger or we older?

Turner   Good to see 'em signin' up.

Bug   They been sayin' they gonna send us more men for two months.

James   Well I'm just the one.

Bug   It's somethin'.

Turner   Things a' lookin' up.

Bug   What time you get here?

Turner   About an hour ago.

Bug   Alright, aint it?

James   Glad to be here.

Bug   Where you been posted before?

James   London.

Bug (*Laughs.*)   I bet yer fuckin' are.

Turner (*Laughs.*)   What a shit hole eh?

Turner and **Bug** *are now quiet.*

Bug   It the way they say?

James   I guess.

Bug   You ain't sure?

James   Never knowed what it like before.

Turner   London's finished.

Bug   No sign a' Recovery there?

Turner   What's it matter?

Bug   Bein' London an' all.

Turner   Manchester's where it's at now.

Bug   Yeah, I know.

Turner   Been improvements there.

Bug   Just askin'.

Turner   Where'd you pick her up?

Bug   About twenty mile from the Sheffield border.

Turner   She have a bag with her?

Bug   Nothin'.

Turner   You pick up a woman with no bag, means she up the spout.

James   You get many that way?

Turner   More than you'd think.

Bug   Them rods in 'em aint guaranteed.

Turner   Dint show up at a clinic or ripped 'em out.

James   Where's she go from here?

Bug   Take her to the train station.

Turner   Same you got off earlier.

Bug   Burns back?

Turner   Nah, better be back here soon, I'm champin' at the bit for tonight.

Bug   Now we got two things to celebrate.

Turner   You comparin' seizin' a knocked-up Illegal to seizin' a pipeline?

Bug *sheepishly shakes his head.*

Turner   Tonight's about the man that had the bollocks to go over there, and had the bollocks to fight. (*Raises his flask.*) We celebratin' the King's bollocks.

Turner *and* **Bug** *belt one back.*

James   Where we goin'?

Bug   When?

James   Tonight? To celebrate.

Turner *and* **Bug** *laugh.*

Turner   Aint goin' nowhere. This here. (*Stops laughing.*)
This is your world. Entire. Sky.

Bug   Mountains.

Turner   Moors.

Bug   Bogs.

Turner   Mud.

Bug   Dirt.

Turner   Cuckoo spit.

Bug   Fox piss.

Turner   Dog shit.

Bug   Cow shit.

Turner   Horse shit.

Bug   Stag skunk.

Turner   And fuck all else.

Burns **enters.**

Turner (*To* **Bug**.)   He's thinkin' about how he can get laid
already.

Burns   Welcome to the Peak.

Burns *and* **James** *shake hands.*

Burns   Burns.

James   James.

Burns   Just got in?

James   Bout an hour ago.

Burns   How was the train up here?

James   Took a while.

Burns   Been some time since I travelled about.

Burns   What's it lookin' like?

James   What d'you mean?

Burns   See any construction work goin' on?

Bug   She in the outbuildin'.

James   Can't say I did.

Burns   Buildin' a homes?

James *shakes his head.*

Turner   He only been sat on a train.

Burns   Repairin' a' roads?

James *shakes his head.*

Turner   Arterial roads have been fixed.

Burns   Nothin' like that?

James *shakes his head.*

Burns   No sign a' Recovery then?

Turner   Priorities s'what they been doin'.

Burns   Thought the Recovery was one.

Beat.

Bug   I got an Illegal.

Burns   Wasn't expectin' yer till tomorrow.

James   When I got inta Manchester there been a freight leavin' early, so I took that.

Burns   Been over to Headquarters whilst you were there?

James   Been given a letter for yer.

Burns   Letter? What kind a' letter?

James *produces the letter.* **Burns** *takes it and reads the envelope.* **James** *steps away.* **Turner** *nods at* **Bug** *for them to give* **Burns** *some space.* **Burns** *opens the envelope and reads the letter. Pause. He laughs. The men turn round.*

Burns   I been put in charge.

Bug *and* **James** *happily step forwards.* **Turner** *stays where he is with a face like a smacked arse.*

Bug (*Pats back.*)   Congratulations.

James (*Shakes hand.*)   Congratulations.

Turner   What's it say?

Burns   You can read it later.

Turner   Like to read it now.

Burns   It goin' up on the kitchen wall.

Mrs Peel *enters.*

Mrs Peel   She's pregnant and she's far gone.

Bug   She aint showin'. You checked?

Mrs Peel   She as wide as a river in spate.

Bug (*Grins.*)   Nothin' worse.

Mrs Peel   When yer boat aint big enough.

Mrs Peel *leaves.*

Burns   There's a train leavin' at eleven. (*To* **Bug**.) You'll just about make it.

Turner   We celebratin' tonight.

Burns   Next trains not for a week.

Turner   What difference does it make?

Burns   No need to drag this thing out.

Turner   Aint as if she gonna drop it in a week.

Burns   Best she goes now.

Turner   He aint gonna get back here till gone three.

Burns   Put her on a horse too.

Turner   I say we vote on it.

Burns   I say what goes on around here now.

Bug nods, **Turner** nods grudgingly. **Burns** leaves.

Bug   He just pissed all over my strawberries.

Bug leaves. **Turner** and **James** watch him go.

Turner   There's no way Stevens would a' done that.

James   Who's Stevens?

Turner   He's the boss round here.

James   Where'd he go?

Turner   Venezuela, with the rest a' 'em. There been eight a' us here to start with.

Turner walks off in the opposite direction to **Bug**.

Turner (Stops.)   You comin'? (Storms off.) We got a war victory to celebrate.

James leaves.

Scene Two

Kitchen. Afternoon.

Megan has mopped the floor, she now rings out the mop. **James** enters, stops as he sees the wet floor between the two of them.

James   Mornin'.

Megan spins round.

Megan   Mornin'.

James   Guess I can't come in here.

They look at the floor . . .

James   How long it gonna take to dry?

Megan   Five minutes.

James   Five?

Megan   Three, maybe.

James   Hard to be exact.

Megan   It tricky to judge.

James   I bet.

They look at each other . . .

James   Come back in five then.

James *makes to leave.*

Megan   Bound to be three by now.

James   Don't seem worth goin'.

Megan   Just to come back again.

Beat.

Megan   You could wait here?

James   I'm not botherin' you?

Megan   I just finished. Well . . . almost.

Megan's *eyes narrow on a supposed blemish on the floor.*

Megan   Missed a bit.

Megan *takes steps forwards with the mop.*

James   It's Megan?

Megan *abandons the idea of mopping.*

Megan   Yeah.

They move towards one another almost imperceptibly.

James   I'm –

Megan   James.

James   Yeah.

They smile, look down at the floor and edge back again in embarrassment.

Megan   What you come here for?

James   Boilin' water. Thought I'd have a shave.

Megan   When's your birthday?

James   Twelfth a' April.

Megan   Just passed.

James *nods.*

Megan   Shame.

James   Why's that?

Megan   You get a bath on your birthday. I had mine too, tenth a' January.

Beat.

Megan   I spent the whole evenin' in mine. Must a' been in it for five hours. Mrs Peel kept bringin' me more hot water each time it went cold and by the end a' it the bath was so full it covered every inch a' me. Then I did somethin' I never done before, to make it special. I opened my eyes in the water, like I was swimmin'. And then, at the very end, I put a jug a' milk in it. (*Shrugs.*) Made my tits soft.

Mrs Peel *enters. She glares at them.*

Megan   He just waitin' for the floor to dry.

Mrs Peel   Looks bone dry to me.

Megan   I'll put that pan a' water on.

James   I'll come back later.

James *makes to leave.*

Mrs Peel   Before you do I'm gonna say a few things about the handlin' a this place that we women see too. Burns may a' told you some a' this already but I'm gonna say it anyway. Cause I like to tell it and Megan here, she like to hear it.

First off. We got plenty to do around here. There aint no idle time for me and her till I give it, aint that right Megan?

Megan *nods.*

Mrs Peel   We got livestock to see to, cleanin' to be done, and meals to be made. You get your breakfast, one cup a' coffee and the pleasure a' me in here at eight. You campin' out and need some food with yer, you come to me about it. Otherwise you get your dinner in here at seven and it'll be served by *me*. You like deer?

James *opens his mouth to speak . . .*

Mrs Peel   Cause it's gonna come fried, boiled, smoked, roasted, dried, burnt and raw. (*Lowers her gaze to his groin.*) Every inch a' it too. I don't do requests or suggestions, come dinner you get what you get. Same as outside we get toiletry supplies once a month. I recommend you use two sheets a' paper for a piss and three for a shit. We don't grow toilet paper, when it's gone it's gone. Any questions?

Mrs Peel*'s eyes narrow onto* **James***'s frame.*

Mrs Peel   You're gonna need to thicken up for the winter. We feel it out here, gets inta your bones, worth it for the clean air though. I'll see to it that I skim the butterfat, get plenty of milk in yer.

James   How'd yer get fresh milk?

Mrs Peel   From a cow's tit.

James   Aint had fresh milk since I been a kid.

Mrs Peel   We set up alright here.

James   You must a' had a farm or somethin' before?

Mrs Peel   There's one more thing for me to tell and I only gonna say it once. I've listened to all the stories a' my generation, then watched 'em get sick or fade away. And it wasn't this world that killed 'em. It was the other. The memory of it. Now. I'm fifty eight, still standin', with nothin' more than a bit a' ring worm. We don't talk about the past here.

Mrs Peel *stares at* **James**. **James** *leaves quietly*. **Megan** *rushes to the stove*.

Mrs Peel   What a' you doin'?

Megan   He forgot the water.

Mrs Peel   He dint forget. He decided he dint want it after all.

Mrs Peel *glares at* **Megan**. **Burns** *enters*.

Burns   Mornin'.

Mrs Peel   Afternoon.

Burns   Suppose it is. We kept yer awake last night?

Mrs Peel   Nothin' disturbs my beauty sleep.

Burns   Cause us men were goin' for it.

Mrs Peel   That aint kept me awake yet.

Burns *sits and picks horse shit off his boot,* **Megan** *watches it fall to the floor.*

Burns   How long for that deer?

Mrs Peel   It aint bled out yet.

Burns   Couple a' hours?

Mrs Peel   I gotta gut her too.

Burns   Three yer say?

Mrs Peel   Then I gotta skin her.

Burns   How long?

Mrs Peel   Four, butcherin's hard work.

Burns   Wanted the boy to have some meat 'for he goes out.

Mrs Peel   Got some dried arse rashers.

Burns   That the best you can do? Still, better than what everyone else has. Can I get a tea?

Megan *looks up from the floor and prepares the tea.*

Mrs Peel   It better, but we could have more.

Mrs Peel *brings out a potato from her apron.*

Mrs Peel (*Sniffs with pride.*)   Now there's this here tater.

Burns *stands,* **Megan** *rushes over,* **Mrs Peel** *guards her potato jealously.*

Mrs Peel   It early, but it right enough.

Megan   I can smell it.

Burns   I can taste it.

Megan   We gonna roast 'em?

Burns   We havin' em mashed.

Megan   Mashed taters and deer!

Burns   How many a' down there?

Mrs Peel   This is it.

Beat.

Burns   You sown one tater?

Mrs Peel   It the only 'en to survive.

Burns *and* **Megan** *walk away.*

Mrs Peel   This here's the beginnin'.

Burns *sits down.*

Mrs Peel   If I can get one I can get more. That plot a' land by the stables, that's the sod I sown this in. That sod would yield a crop.

Burns   We an outpost here, Mrs Peel. Not a farm.

Mrs Peel   Most a' the works preparin' the land, but then we'd be set.

Burns   Need a plough to do that.

Mrs Peel   Spades'd do the work of a plough, could get some vegetable plots out a' it too.

Burns   You and Megan'd be spadin' for weeks.

Mrs Peel   Can't wait that long, humidity'll get em like it done before. If we had some extra hands with us . . .

Burns   I aint puttin' my men on a shovel.

Mrs Peel   Me and her'd tend to it after that. Barn's good for storin' what we'd harvest.

Burns   I aint sayin' it again.

Mrs Peel   We could be self sufficient, no more tinned rations.

Burns   Answers no.

Pause. **Mrs Peel** *brings out the potato and rubs it.*

Mrs Peel   See how the skin's comin' off?

Burns doesn't look at Mrs Peel.

Mrs Peel   Skin aint had the chance to set firm.

Mrs Peel *sets the potato on the table before* **Burns**.

Mrs Peel   Means it's new.

Turner, *worse for wear, and* **Bug** *enter.*

Mrs Peel   Brand new.

Burns *now looks at the potato.*

Turner   I got a head as bad as a bastard. Coffee on?

Megan   Doin' it now.

Bug   Is that a spud?

Turner   Need somethin' to settle my gut.

Bug   How come we've got spuds?

Megan   Fetch you some milk?

Turner *ignores* **Megan**'*s offer and looks at the potato on the table.*

Turner   Fried taters.

Turner *turns to* **Bug**.

Bug   Fried deer.

Bug *turns to* **Turner**.

Turner   Fried egg.

Bug   Tin a' beans.

The realisation hits them at the same time.

Bug   That's a full English breakfast!

Turner   Kiss me quick I'm comin'!

Mrs Peel   Tater aint for breakfast.

Mrs Peel *shoves the potato in her apron.*

Turner   Why, what a' we havin'?

Mrs Peel   I make it way past eight.

Turner   I make it your job to cater for us.

Beat. **Mrs Peel** *lights the stove.*

Bug   Where's James?

Turner   He up and around.

Bug   Shall I go get him?

Turner   What a' you askin' me for?

Bug *walks out of the kitchen.*

Bug (*Hollers.*) James! . . . (*Hollers.*) James! . . . (*Hollers.*)
James!

Bug *comes back into the kitchen.*

Turner   I got a tongue as dry as a horse's hoof, that coffee
ready?

Megan   Bringin' it now.

Megan *brings the coffee to the table as* **James** *enters.*

Bug (*To* **James**.)   Breakfast.

James   Thought I'd missed it.

James *sits at the table.*

Bug   Slept well?

James   Yeah, I did.

Turner   With them dogs barkin'?

James   Too tired to hear anythin'.

Turner   You must a' heard 'em, Burns?

Burns   What?

Turner   Dogs goin' at it last night. I say we head over to
Edale, pitch up there for a couple a' days.

Bug *agrees.*

James   Where's Edale?

Turner   North east a' here, about twenty mile. Nothin' to it
really, just a straight mile a' cottages runnin' through.

Bug   It been empty a long time, way before the orders
came to leave. Been a tourist spot before, droves a' walkers
passin' through on weekends, kind a' place southerners
retired too.

Turner   What it is is a prime spot for Illegals.

Bug   We check the cottages for any sign a' 'em, blankets, smuts still alive, empty tinned food cans where the sauce aint turned.

Turner   They hole up in 'em before makin' their way just north a' there to the Pennine Way, leads all the way up to the Scottish border. Most a' the time that's where the cunts a' headin', Scotland.

Bug   Thinkin' it better in the north.

Turner   Sometimes I reckon the border restrictions should be lifted for a week.

Mrs Peel *and* **Megan** *bring in four plates of a dismal breakfast.*

Turner   Let all the Civilians in cities and settlements go where ever the fuck they want and see it pretty much the same everywhere. After that they'd be back in their pens and the cunts'd stay put, no more Illegals. (*Grins with a mouthful.*) But then we'd be out of a' job.

Beat.

Turner   That alright with you Burns if we do Edale?

Burns (*Nods.*)   Do a circle on the way back by Kinder Scoutt.

Turner   You takin' James out with you or he comin' with us?

Burns   Me and him's stayin' about here.

Turner   Showed him what there is yesterday.

Burns   There's some work to be done.

Turner   What work?

Burns   Seein' to that plot a' land by the stables.

Mrs Peel *looks over at* **Burns** *and* **Turner** *sees her.*

Burns   Preparin' it for a crop.

Bug   More spuds?

Burns   Needs to be weeded and spaded first.

Bug   All a' it?

Burns   Me and James'll start her off.

Bug   That's a lot a' shovellin'.

Burns   Youse can take over when you get back, be done in a week or so.

Turner *stands.*

Bug   Where you goin'?

Turner   To do my job.

Turner *walks off.* **Bug** *stands.*

Burns   See you in a couple a' days.

Bug *nods and leaves.*

Burns   Any good at shovellin' James?

James   Can't say I done it before.

Mrs Peel *enters to clear the plates.*

Burns   S'like bein' the batsman in cricket.

James   Can't say I been that either.

Burns *and* **James** *leave.*

Burns   It's all in the kneel.

Mrs Peel   Burns?

Burns *stops before he leaves turns to* **Mrs Peel**. *Beat.*

Mrs Peel   New boy been in here this mornin'. He been real excited to know we got a cow, way I see it he aint had his hands around a teat in a long time. Make sure he knows that milkin' the cow aint his job round here.

Mrs Peel *leaves.*

Scene Three

Peak. Night.

Turner *is sat staring into the small fire.* **Bug** *approaches* **Turner** *from behind. The horses are heard to stir occasionally.*

Bug (*Sheepishly.*)   Turner . . .

Turner   What?

Beat.

Turner   What you forgot this time?

Bug   The tarp.

Turner   What a' we gonna do now?

Bug   We could go back?

Turner   I aint goin' back.

Bug   I could go back.

Turner   Fuck the tarp.

Bug   Fuck the tarp?

Turner   Fuck the tarp. Fuck the rain. Fuck the land. Fuck Burns.

Bug (*Grins.*)   Thought you was pissed at me.

Turner   And fuck you.

Bug (*Still grinning.*)   But you aint.

Turner   Aint you pissed about it?

Bug   Yeah, I'm pissed. But. Way I see it, I only gotta be pissed for three days.

Turner   Three days?

Bug   Four max.

Turner   We supposed to be patrollin' this here bastard peak, and now there's just two a' us doin' it.

Bug   We'll be four by the end a' the week.

Turner   By then we could a' lost out on god knows how many Illegals.

Bug   Aint as if we pickin' 'em up every week, Turn.

Turner   You know why? Cause they fear us. They fear us, Bug. That's why.

Bug *looks out.*

Turner   This whole gardenin' thing, it dint come from Burns.

Bug   What d'you mean?

Turner   That old rope, Peel. It her idea.

Bug   Wouldn't mind havin' some spuds.

Turner   She sowin' more than that.

Bug   Reckon we'll get peas?

Turner   Would you stop thinkin' about your gut and think about what's goin' on here. Aint Burns puttin' us on a shovel, it Peel, a civilian. I like Burns, don't get me wrong, he been a good soldier, done his fair share a' tours. But that was some time ago, this last three year he been lookin' up at the moon through a whiskey bottle waitin' for his boy to come back. He aint got the grit to do the job, s'all I'm sayin'.

Beat.

Turner   Put some food on?

Bug   Aint hungry yet.

Turner   Me neither

Bug   You know what I been thinkin' about?

Turner   Gettin' laid?

Bug   Yeah, but somethin' else too.

Turner *looks blank.*

Bug   Keep thinkin' about that stag.

Turner   Why?

Bug   I don't know.

Turner   So what you talkin' about it for?

Bug   I don't know.

Beat.

Bug   Never seen a stag bitten like that.

Turner   Seen it before.

Bug   Whatever it was knew what it was doin', straight for the jugular.

Turner   What d'you mean: whatever it was?

Bug   I don't know.

Turner   Told you a dog done it.

Bug   It was a big bastard too.

Turner   Fuckin' three dogs then.

Bug   Not an organ left.

Turner   How many times has one of them stray dogs come at you? Them dogs have spent most a' their life sprawled on a rug in front of a TV fartin'. But with all that gone they're wild.

Bug   Yeah, you're right.

Beat.

Bug   Never seen a dog this far inta the Peak.

Turner   And I never had such a borin' conversation.

Beat.

Bug   Haven't pitched in this spot for a while.

Turner   Couple a' week maybe.

Bug   Had this dream, last time we were sleepin' here. Not really a dream cause I was awake, sleepy eyed kind a' thing. The whole place was lit. Burnin'. Red with fire. Some trees fallin'. The ground scorched . . .

Turner   And then what?

Bug   (*Shrugs.*)   Nothin'.

Scene Four

Stables. Evening.

Megan *is laid on her back staring upwards.* **James** *enters.*

James   Evenin'.

Megan *jumps to her feet.*

Megan   Evenin'.

James   Came to check the tack for my horse.

Megan   Which one been given?

James   Sheets.

Beat.

James   What a' you doin'?

Megan   I'm bein' alone.

Beat.

James   You come here to do that?

Megan   Huhum.

Beat.

Megan   Mrs Peel don't tend to come here. She don't like the horses much, especially Mince. He been eating her sage bush. Sheets kicked her in the gut. But she was alright about that.

James   Guess I'll be goin' then.

Megan   I don't mind sharin' this space. I could just sit here alone, sit here sharin' it, s'all the same to me – you like stars?

James   I guess.

Megan   Want a' see some?

James   Alright.

Megan   S'why I'm always in this spot so I can see 'em.

James *edges forwards to where* **Megan** *stands.*

Megan   I sometimes sit outside when you all sleepin' and look at 'em too. It's so quiet and dark. Never no planes in the sky, no headlights, lights from windows. Just them stars and me. You know that the stars a' suns?

James *shakes his head.*

Megan   Sun's just the closet one to us is all. Mrs Peel told me that. Told me that everyone a' them stars is gonna die sometime and same goes for ours. But before it dies, a long time before it dies, it gonna cook us to a crisp and boil all the water away. You know that?

James *shakes his head.*

Megan   She told me that the moon's done for too. Every year it moves further away and there'll come a time when it won't support us no more, we're gonna drop like a sack a' taters. You know that?

James *shakes his head.*

Megan   Don't really matter anyway cause the sun'll cook us first.

Beat.

James   Know how to find the North star.

Megan   Mrs Peel don't know that.

James   There's seven bright stars in the shape of a saucepan. You find the saucepan and take the edge a' it that's furthest away from the handle. You draw a line from the star at the base a' the pan to the star at the rim. You extend it about five times. That leads you to another saucepan. A smaller one. You take the edge a' the smaller saucepan's handle that's furthest away from the pan and you found the North Star. Drop a vertical line from the North Star to the horizon and that's north.

Megan *is lost yet impressed.*

James   Orientation was part a' my trainin'. Taught to orientate ourselves without a compass. Had to learn to memorize co-ordinates. Told never to fold a map any other way than it already folded. That way you give nothin' about the operation away. I liked that part a' it, learnin' I mean.

Megan   How much schoolin' you had?

James   Till I was twelve.

Megan   Same here.

James   We must be the same age then.

Megan   I like learnin' too.

Beat.

James   Show you some tactical hand signals if you want?

Megan   What a' they?

James   Stuff you do to not give the operation away.

Megan's *game.*

James (*Raise his arm clenches his fist.*)   Hold.

Megan (*Does the same.*)   Hold.

James (*Crosses his arms across his chest.*)   Obstacle.

Megan (*Does the same.*)   Obstacle.

James (*Raises his arm, points the finger, rotates it.*)   Regroup.

Megan (*Does the same.*)   Regroup.

James (*Hand into a spy hole.*)   Look out.

Megan (*Does the same.*)   Look out.

James (*Cups his ear.*)   Say again.

Megan (*Does the same.*)   Say again.

James   Best stop there, gets confusin' if you do too many.

Megan   Never been someone my age here before.

James   Security's always been full a' the other generation. But since most a' thems gone overseas it left an openin' for us. Now that we old enough to do it. I signed up a year ago.

Beat.

Megan   So now you got health care.

James   Yeah. Not that I need it, I aint got nothin'.

Megan   Good to have it.

James   I guess.

Megan   Get more rations too.

James   When I was outside, here we eatin' the same.

Megan   Bigger livin' quarters for you.

James   Aint done it for none a' that.

Megan (*Nods.*)   Just wanted to be in the Security.

James   First time I had a choice in somethin'. Everythin' else been decided for me. Figured, if I'm gonna be drafted as well, I'd rather choose it than it get me. So that's what I done. Some a' them I knew dint speak to me after I done it. But. They don't speak much to each other outside anyway. This is the most I talked in a long time. Gonna get me in bother, like it did this mornin' with Mrs Peel.

Megan   She always like that.

James   Should a' known better.

Megan   Should be able to ask things sometimes.

The horses are heard to whinny. **Megan** *becomes alert.*

James   I should be goin'.

Megan   Probably just a mouse stirred 'em.

James   You sure Mrs Peel aint gonna come?

Megan   Last time I seen her she was pullin' whiskers out a' her chin and nose. She don't tend to come out a' our room after she been doin' that. This here's my free time, don't get much a' that.

James   She worked you hard on that shovel today.

Megan   She always workin' me, even when there's nothin' needs doin', but it good for me. When there was more men here I been busy most a' the time but when they went away I been told I was gonna be sent back to my old quarters and put to work in the refinery.

James   How come you stayed?

(*Beat.*)

Megan   Turner, he put in a good word for me.

James   Don't seem like him.

Megan   Here a bit like where I grew up, dint have horses a' nothin' but reminds me a' it sometimes . . .

James   Thought you dint talk about the past here?

Megan   I don't do everythin' Mrs Peel tells me. Today I chucked a handful a seeds down the toilet. Yesterday I tipped coffee grinds inta the compost like I been told too, but I slung in a tea bag, like I been told not too. Day before I spotted a hare munchin' away at her first ever courgette flower and I stood by and let it eat it down to the core. Last month I took a knife and made a gash in her mosquito nettin', and sure enough she been bit. And for a year I been watchin' a vine slowly spreadin' itself on top a' the spade I hid and I let it keep on growin' like toe nails on a corpse.

Burns (*Offstage.*)   James?

James   I gotta go.

Megan   He just callin' he aint comin' here.

Burns (*Offstage.*)   James?

James   I should go.

James *walks away, stops, turns around*.

James   Maybe see you in here again?

Megan   I don't mind sharin' this space.

Megan *sits*.

Megan   S'all same to me.

James *leaves.* **Megan** *smiles*.

Scene Five

Kitchen. Afternoon.

Mrs Peel *and* **Megan** *are before the table which is covered in seeds.* **James** *and* **Burns** *are bringing boxes of supplies into the kitchen.*

Mrs Peel   Potatoes, peas, beans are all the seed for their kind, cucumbers and most fruit contain the seed within 'em, we'll pick 'em out. Reason there's so many different kinds is, where one will fail another can still succeed. They're not all gonna' survive. Nature knows that, spreads it chances. When pickin' leaves and mushrooms you gotta be careful that they aint poisonous. A rule a' thumb I swear by is if you don't recognize it or it's got a dick don't trust it. (*Glares at* **James**.) Get rid a' it.

Burns *sits on a box and decanters the whiskey bottle into his flask.*

Mrs Peel (*To* **Burns**.)   One a' your dogs has been in here last night and had itself a free for all. I had a deer's tongue in a little dish over there, marinadin' in some vinegar and garlic over night –

Burns   Vinegar and garlic?

Mrs Peel   I don't appreciate feedback on my cookin'. I walk in here, dish is tipped over, and No Tongue. Best bit too.

Burns   Yer can say that again.

Mrs Peel *dislikes* **Burns**'s *tone and lets him know it.*

Burns   I'll tell 'em to be more careful when tyin' 'em up at night.

Mrs Peel   Damn good kick up the goolies is what it needs.

Burns   You got one less bag a' flour and no coffee.

Mrs Peel   You got tea?

Burns *nods.*

Mrs Peel   You checked it? Cause last time they diddled yer.

Burns   Everythin' else is there.

Mrs Peel *shifts her attention back to* **Megan**.

Mrs Peel   Most a' what you gonna be doin' is sowin', waterin' and harvestin'. But you'll need to have the eye a' the hawk about you at all times. Why? Cause you're on the look out for Fungus . . .

James *enters with the last of the supplies.*

Mrs Peel   And he comes in all shapes and guises. Mould, mildew, black spot. You see any sign a' Fungus you come to me.

James *looks at the seeds on the table.*

Mrs Peel   You see a bird pullin' at the tops a' my spring opinions, a hare helpin' itself to my cabbages, a slug suckin' up my salad (*turns on* **James**) what d'you do?

James   I come to you?

Mrs Peel   Wrong.

Mrs Peel *edges towards* **James**.

Mrs Peel   You nip it in the bud right there and then. You take your hand! a rock! a shovel! and you do whatever it takes.

Burns   Any chance a' some breakfast? Been up and out at dawn gettin' this lot.

Mrs Peel   Megan, make Burns some breakfast.

Mrs Peel *starts putting the supplies away.* **Megan** *makes the breakfast. Secret glances are shared between* **James** *and* **Megan** *in the silence. Burns switches the radio on.*

Radio   The government has announced today that more vouchers will be distributed (*Tunes . . .*) Intervals of showers (*Tunes . . .*) Terror and dread fell upon them by the might of your arm. (*Tunes . . .*) And finally may we remind Civilians that there is a strong UV warning tomorrow . . . (*Tunes . . . crazy sermon.*) The Spirit of the Lord God is upon me! –

Burns *switches it off.*

Mrs Peel   Evangelicals, nuttier than a squirrel's fart.

Burns   Spoutin' their horse shit on every network.

James   Same on the streets too.

Burns   Man wants to eat his breakfast and listen to the news.

Mrs Peel   Aint broadcast nothin' true in years.

Turner *and* **Bug** *enter, sweating and soiled from shovelling, they zoom in on the supplies.*

Burns   They don't say the half a' it, I know that.

Turner (*Pulls out the whiskey.*)   Arh yes!

James   Dint even announce that bomb in Leeds.

Everyone turns to **James**. *Beat.*

Turner   What?

Burns   Bomb in Leeds?

Turner   What did you just say?

Bug   Leeds has been bombed!

James   No.

Turner   What did you just say!

Beat.

James (*Quietly.*)   That bomb in Leeds at Security Headquarters. Thought you knew.

Burns   When did this happen?

James   Four . . . five week ago.

Bug   Four, five week ago!

Turner   A' you takin' the piss out a' us?

James   What?

Turner   I said a' you takin' the piss out a' us?

James   No.

Turner   Think you can say bullshit and we'll believe you?

Burns   What happened?

James   A bomb went off –

Turner   We know that!

Burns   Who set it off?

James   Civilians.

Pause.

Bug   Civilians?

Burns   How'd they get inta Headquarters?

James   They blew off the gates.

Turner   How'd they get a bomb?

James   They made it.

Burns   And then what?

James   They sieged the Headquarters.

Beat.

Turner   Sieged?

Burns   How many were they?

James   Eight.

Bug   Eight Civilians sieged a' Headquarters?

Turner   What were the Security doin'!

James (*Shrugs.*)   Sleepin' mostly.

Turner   You tryin' to be funny?

James   It was night, they took 'em by surprise and opened fire.

Bug   What?

James   They had guns, worked in an arms factory.

Turner   And what? We payin' 'em with arms now!

Bug   They'll a smuggled 'em out.

Turner   I know that.

Burns   What was the damage?

James   Communication lines destroyed, women's records burnt, twelve Security dead.

Beat.

Turner   What happened to the eight?

James   Six dead and two executed.

Bug   Why dint we know about this?

Turner   How did you find out?

James   Been told, word a' it spread amongst the Security.

Turner   But nothin' official came through?

James *shakes his head.*

Burns   Playin' down the threat.

Bug   What d'you mean?

Burns   There was always gonna come a day when they'd rise.

Turner (*To* **Bug**.)   Eight dead, dint rise at all.

Burns   It just the beginnin'.

Turner (*To* **Bug**.)   They failed.

Burns   They'll do it again.

Turner (*To* **Burns**.)   It one incident.

Burns   You call that an incident?

Turner   It dint change nothin'.

Bug   Twelve Security dead?

Turner   We soldiers, soldiers die.

Bug   Yeah but overseas.

Burns   War just got closer.

Turner   Ah for fuck's sake, eight Civilians!

Bug   You think it gonna lead to that?

Turner (*To* **Bug**.)   Would you shut up!

Burns   It been eight but more will follow.

Turner   They aint never fought back.

Burns   When the elections were cancelled they did.

Turner   And after that day they never done it again.

Pause. **Turner***,* **Burns** *and* **Bug** *become very aware of* **Mrs Peel***.*

Turner   What did the Civilians a' Leeds do James, after this here *siege*?

James   What d'you mean?

Turner   They dint run on over there and join in?

James   No.

Turner   They dint try again in the weeks that followed?

James (*Shakes his head.*)

Turner   No. They've accepted how things are, same as they accepted how things were gonna be all them years ago, and they aint never done nothin' about it between. (*To* **Bug***.*) Bring some a' that whiskey out with us.

Bug *lifts out a bottle.*

James   They were young, the eight.

Turner   Makes no difference.

Bug *and* **Turner** *make to leave.*

James   Think they angry.

Turner   Eight angry teenagers . . . (*Whistles.*) the times we livin' in.

James   Weren't teenagers, been about my age.

Turner   Now I'm really shittin' it.

Burns   It gonna be us they'll come for.

Bug   But we're doin' our job.

Turner   We're here cause the country needed us to be.

Burns   Weren't meant to become this.

Turner   Everythin' we done had to be done.

Bug   What were the government supposed to do?

Turner   We aint here cause a' some ideology.

Burns   Oh I know that, there are no ideas anymore.

Turner   There's the Recovery!

Beat.

Turner   And we're here to ensure that that happens.

Turner *makes to leave.*

Burns   We've got the same debt as a third world country, Turner.

Turner   We are no third world country.

Burns   We could a' prepared for what was to come whilst we still had the money to do so, but no, no, he signed us up to war and debt.

Turner   Don't blame him when it was every other prick in office before him.

Burns   Debt to fight wars that aint even ours.

Turner   Aint ours? The cunts turned the tap off!

Burns   We did not need to join them. And now we'll never be free. We can't pay them back, and they don't want us too. They'd rather have us like this . . . a colony.

Turner   You're gettin' our enemies mixed up.

Burns   They are not our ally.

Turner   And they're not our enemy. Take one look at history and it'll tell you that, yeah, they can be a nasty cunt, but not to us. They always been on our side and when this is over they'll help us with the Recovery.

Burns   There's no Recovery!

Turner   This is England!

Burns   This is not England!

Turner   Then what's your Brian fightin' for if it's not his country?

Burns   My lads not fightin' for his country.

Turner *walks away.*

Burns   He's fightin' for a pipe.

Turner *storms off and* **Bug** *follows.*

Burns   They're fightin' for whatever's left!

Burns *belts back a long drink. Silence.*

Mrs Peel   Like strawberry pie, Burns?

Burns   What?

Mrs Peel   You like strawberry pie?

Burns   Never had it.

Mrs Peel   Megan, fetch me a tin a' strawberries for Burn's pie.

Megan *leaves.* **Mrs Peel** *looks at* **James**, *he leaves.*

Mrs Peel   Ask you a question, Burns?

Burns   Everybody else has.

Mrs Peel   Why a' you in the Security?

Burns   Ask me another.

Mrs Peel   You regret it?

Beat.

Burns   My granddad was a coal miner. Started on the shovel at seventeen. Worked down there till he was fifty five. Lungs packed up when he was fifty nine. He was not a morbid man but over the years he often spoke about his death. Said, I spent most a' my life underground, and when I'm dead, don't put me back down there. (*Turns to* **Mrs Peel**) We buried him.

Mrs Peel   Why?

Burns   Couple a' month before his funeral, he goes to someone else's. My grandma's sat with him in the crematorium. The sad music starts, the doors raised, the coffin gets half way in. My granddad walks out. Grandma leaves when its over, finds him waitin' outside. First thing he says to her, I spent most a' my life down there, and when I'm dead, I'm goin' back down there.

Mrs Peel   Which one does that answer?

Burns   Both.

They share a smile. **Mrs Peel** *walks away.*

Burns   How about whippin' up some cream for my pie Mrs P?

Mrs Peel   I don't do requests or suggestions, Burns. Nor do I do abbreviations. I'm Mrs Peel, always.

Megan *enters with the tin.*

Mrs Peel   Pie'll be ready this evenin'.

Burns *leaves.*

Megan   They never shouted like that.

Mrs Peel   They ballin' all the time.

Megan   Never shouted about them things. Think he said, should a' prepared. You been told what would happen.

Mrs Peel   What a' you sayin' Megan?

Megan *gives the tin to* **Mrs Peel**.

Megan   This pie just for Burns?

Mrs Peel   He havin' the first slice.

Megan   Can I have the second?

Mrs Peel   You can have a' slice too.

Megan   Can I help make it?

Mrs Peel   You wash the slaughter house floor first.

Megan *nods with pursed lips.*

Mrs Peel   You get their uniforms in a tub.

Megan *nods with pursed lips.*

Mrs Peel   You come and tell me then you can roll the pastry.

Megan nods, **Mrs Peel** *turns away.*

James *is about to enter –* **Megan** *shoots her arm up and makes a fist (hold signal) and* **James** *steps back.* **Mrs Peel** *turns to* **Megan**, *who still has her hand in the air.*

Mrs Peel   What a' you doin'?

Megan   Just killed a fly.

Mrs Peel   Open up that hand.

Megan *slowly opens her palm.*

Megan   Thought I killed a fly. (*Looks about.*) It gone.

Mrs Peel *turns away.* **Megan** *looks for* **James** *but he isn't there.*

Megan   Skin a' my hands is cracked and sore.

Mrs Peel   Rub a little butter on 'em.

Megan   Need more than butter.

Mrs Peel   Butter's what you got.

Megan   Put some on my face the other night.

Mrs Peel   You been abusin' that butter?

Megan   Don't want my face to wrinkle.

Mrs Peel   You use it for cracks and sores only.

Megan *sees* **James**'s *head – she crosses her arms across her chest* (*obstacle.*) **Mrs Peel** *turns to* **Megan**, *who still has her arms across her chest.* **Mrs Peel** *stands staring at* **Megan**. **Megan** *moves her hands about her arms as if they were a lovers.* **Mrs Peel** *looks at* **Megan** *like she's loosing the plot.* **Megan** *finally stops.*

Megan (*Shrugs.*)   Nice to hold yourself sometimes.

Mrs Peel   I'm gonna go and grab hold a' some sheep balls.

Mrs Peel *leaves.* **James** *enters.*

James   She comin' back?

Megan   She gonna' be a while.

James   You sure?

Megan   She got her hands full.

James   Remembered the tactical signals pretty well.

Megan   I did, didn't I.

Beat.

Megan   Have to teach me somethin' else now.

James   Like what?

Megan   Have to think a' somethin'.

Beat.

James   Want a' know some lateral thinkin'?

Megan   Don't have to be from trainin'.

James   Don't know much else.

Megan   Dint sound like that earlier.

James   Burns and Turner done the talkin'.

Megan   You been the one they askin'.

James   Dint have much of an opinion about it.

Megan   You had the facts.

James   Sat there listenin' mostly s'what I done. Reminded me a' when I used to go meetin's with my dad. It been after the Breakdown that. There'd be about fifty a' us, standin' or sittin' in a pokey terrace. I just been a kid, been there listenin'. But the rest a' 'em been talkin' and shoutin' all night. Like I say, been after the Breakdown, could a' made a bonfire out a' their anger. Been that way for about a year, meetin's twice a week. Then he started goin' less, wasn't the only one. He been too tired after his shift or worried that the Security, they'd break up meeting sometimes, would have him down as trouble. He still talked about it all in the evenin's after the news, but he done it with my mum. She always sittin' there quiet. Dint cry no more. When he been promoted to foreman in the factory he stopped goin'. Last meetin' we went to there been a dozen a' us and it finished before the lights went out. (*Shifts.*) This past year I been the one who's breakin' up meetin's . . . they still have 'em in terraces, but they younger who go to 'em . . . aint been any less a' 'em each time we went back . . . I'm talkin' again . . . shouldn't get used to it.

Megan   Aint a bad thing.

James   Good thing. That's why.

Beat.

Megan   When I planted the rhubarb Mrs Peel told me she was gonna make a rhubarb juice with it when it was ready. I never had rhubarb juice before but she told me it's like apple juice but better and I really like apple juice. We started savin' some sugar aside at the beginnin' a' every month for it and after waitin' a whole year it was ready. It was one a' the best things I ever tasted. I had a cup a' it every day for ten days. And then it was gone and I got upset about that. I cried. The next year when the rhubarb was ready Mrs Peel dint make no juice with it. She boiled it up and made me eat it with no sugar for two weeks. That was a long time ago now.

Rhubarb's gonna be ready next month and Mrs Peel promised me she gonna make juice with it. When it's gone it's gone. I know that now. I just have to enjoy it whilst its there.

Megan *and* **James** *lean towards one another – a strange rasping noise.*

James   What's that?

Megan (*Softly.*)   Sheep.

Megan *and* **James** *lean further, until they are inches apart – a distressed rasping noise.*

James   Don't sound like sheep.

Megan (*Softly.*)   Mrs Peel's castratin' 'em s'why.

James *jerks backwards.*

James   I gotta go.

James *rushes off, stops.*

James   Tonight?

Megan (*Beams.*)   Tonight.

James *leaves.*

Scene Six

Peak. Sunset.

Turner *and* **Bug** *are sat eating from their tinned cans in silence.*

Bug   I tell yer about that seagull? Don't think I did. When I dropped that deer, eight . . . nine days ago now, anyway, deer's on the ground. I'm makin' my way to it when out a' nowhere a seagull comes down and pecks out the deer's eyeball. If I'd a' been any longer gettin' to it it'd gone straight for its arse hole (*Half laughs.*) . . .

Turner   No fish for 'em.

Beat.

Bug   First thing you said since we been out here.

Turner   Thinkin', s'all.

Bug   Man can think aloud.

Turner   Aint ready in my head yet.

Bug   I say stuff that aint ready all the time.

Turner   I know. S'why I aint.

Beat.

Bug   Thinkin' about what Burns said?

Turner   Nope.

Bug   I been thinkin' about what Burns said.

Beat.

Bug   Pretty fucked, aint it?

Turner   Nope.

Beat.

Bug   How's that.

Turner   I'm sick a' talkin' about. Sick a' thinkin' about it. Don't even matter to me anymore. Recovery or no Recovery, it aint gonna make no difference to me and what I'm gonna do. I served my country. I done my duty. I aint doin' it . . . I aint.

Bug   What?

Turner   Fuck 'em. Fuck 'em all.

Bug   What a' you talkin' about?

Turner   I'm gonna find myself an abandoned farm. Fix it up. And stay the fuck there.

(*Beat.*)

Could be there too if yer wanted.

(*Beat.*)

Turner   World already got smaller, and it can get even smaller for me. It can get as small as a farm and a couple a' acres a' land. It can empty itself a' everybody till there's just me and you left. It can burn itself to the ground around us.

Beat.

Turner   Man can't be alone. (*Glances at* **Bug**.) I know what time a' day it is with you and . . . you do me. Way I see it, we'd get along fine anywhere's.

Beat.

Turner   Anyway, that's what I'm gonna do.

Pause.

Turner   What you gone quiet for!

Bug   I'm just listenin'.

Turner   Told you I dint want a' say nothin'!

Turner *stands.*

Turner   Said it wrong cause you're fuckin' quizzin' me.

Bug   I aint quizzin' you.

Turner   You're fuckin' quizzin' me all the fuckin' time.

Bug   Ah, fuck this.

Turner   Yeah, fuck you.

Bug *walks away. Both men stand opposite, backs turned. Pause.*

Bug   Prick.

Turner   Wanker.

Bug   Cock.

Turner   Cock sucker.

Bug   Cunt.

Turner   Cunty bollocks.

Bug   Spunk ball.

Turner   Spunk ball?

Bug   Spunk ball.

Turner   Inventive.

They take out their flasks, swig one back.

Bug   Reddest sky I seen tonight.

Turner   Reckon it's gonna rain?

Bug   Can't never tell.

Turner *and* **Bug** *become alert – the clack and ricochet of stag's antlers.*

Bug   Stags.

Turner *looks away, but* **Bug** *continues to stare out.*

Turner   Lucky bastards.

Bug   They aint ruttin'.

Turner   Next life I'm comin' back as a stag.

Bug   They chargin' forwards, they fightin'.

Turner   Fuck me they even get foreplay.

Turner *sits down by the fire.*

Bug   What you been sayin' earlier.

Turner   Forget about that.

Bug   Makes sense to me. Never thought about it but soon as you said it, had it all figured in my head. I even seen the place, Turn. Everythin' just fell inta place . . . Except for one thing.

Turner   What?

Bug   How we gonna get it?

Turner   Need to think it over.

Bug   You said it'd be an abandoned farm?

Turner *doesn't answer, he drinks from his flask.*

Bug   Means it'd be outside a' the restrictions.

Turner   They all been emptied years before that.

Bug   Don't matter if it were before or after.

Turner *stands, shifts about agitated.*

Turner   Restrictions don't apply to us.

Bug   They would if we weren't in the Security no more.

Turner *becomes still.*

Turner   Restrictions aint gonna be forever. (*Turns to* **Bug**.) Gotta lift 'em some time.

Bug *nods and they look away from each other.*

Bug   Where we settin' up for the night?

Turner   Castleton.

Turner *picks up his rifle*

Bug   Had this thing happen there.

Turner   What thing?

Bug   Felt somethin' watchin' me.

Turner   What'd you mean?

Bug   Even though I was sleepin', I knew it was there.

Turner *walks off.*

Turner (*Calls back.*)   I've dreamt a pussy and woke up fuckin' tastin' it.

Bug   Wasn't a dream.

Turner *has left.* **Bug** *picks up his rifle and turns to leave. He stands motionless as he sees the figure of a man in the distance. The man's head is lowered and he wears a crown made of stag's antlers, smeared in blood. The man drops to his knees. A wind rises.*

Scene Seven

Slaughter room. Morning. The wind howls.

A deer bound by its back legs hangs down from an iron grip. The bucket directly below it collects the blood as it bleeds out. **Megan** *is holding the knife at the deer,* **Mrs Peel** *stands behind her.*

Mrs Peel   Start at her crotch and take it all the way to her breast.

Megan *draws the line with the blade.*

Mrs Peel   Don't show her all a' yer blade, just the tip, give enough to get under her hide.

Megan *brings the blade back.*

Mrs Peel   You do the same thing again but this time you givin' it more, give her a half inch, that'll open her up. Don't get carried away, cause if you do, you gonna be in her stomach.

Burns *enters.*

Burns   Nearly got killed makin' my way here.

Mrs Peel (*To* **Megan**.)   Start steelin' the blade.

Burns   Some loose tiles fell not more than a foot away from me.

Mrs Peel   Not seen a wind like this before, couple a' fence posts heaved themselves clean out a' the soil durin' the night.

Mrs Peel *sees that* **Burns** *has been drinking.*

Mrs Peel   Need somethin' Burns?

Burns   Listened to the radio this mornin'?

Mrs Peel   We graftin' from since six nowadays.

Burns   King's dead.

Megan *stops steeling the blade.*

Burns   Died over there last night. They've lost the stronghold. They aint bringin' anyone back.

Mrs Peel *watches* **Burns** *drink from his flask.*

Burns   Yer gonna have two less mouths to feed as a' tomorrow.

Mrs Peel   Who been drafted?

Burns   Bug and James.

Mrs Peel   They bein' replaced?

Burns   No one to replace 'em. They sendin' thousands to Venezuela. It just gonna be me and Turner out here.

The wind shrieks.

Burns   Damn wind.

Mrs Peel   Somethin' cooler is settin' in.

Burns   You reckon its here to stay?

Mrs Peel   I do.

Beat.

Mrs Peel   Anythin' else?

Burns   Put a half bottle a' whiskey under the sink yesterday.

Mrs Peel   Already seen it.

Burns   You don't miss a trick, Mrs Peel.

Mrs Peel   I got twenty twenty vision, Burns.

Turner *storms in followed by* **Bug**.

Turner   We need to talk!

Burns   No point talkin' to me about it.

Bug   Come on, Turn.

Turner   Why aint I goin'?

Burns   I don't decide who goes and who stays.

Turner   But you can do somethin' about it.

Bug   It been decided, Turn.

Turner   He aint goin' without me.

Burns   Nothin' I can do about it.

Turner   This is bullshit.

Burns   Turner! I wouldn't hesitate in sendin' you instead of that boy if I could.

Turner   I want to go!

Bug   It aint up to him.

Turner   I'm leavin' tomorrow.

Bug   You can't do that.

Turner   I'm takin' James's place.

Bug   They won't allow it.

Turner   What the fuck's he gonna do out there? He don't know shit. He aint gonna last a week.

Bug   You know the drill, Turn.

Turner   Would you shut up.

Bug   Ah fuck this.

Turner   Yeah fuck you.

Megan (*From the gut.*)   Stop!

Everyone turns to **Megan**. *Pause.*

Megan (*Trembling.*)   I got a deer to skin.

James *enters,* **Megan** *turns away.*

Mrs Peel   What d'you want?

James   Hares a' eatin' tops a' your courgettes.

Mrs Peel   What did I tell you! Don't just stand there –

James   There's too many a' 'em.

Mrs Peel (*Gravely.*)   How many?

James   Five.

Mrs Peel *draws her blade and breath.*

Mrs Peel   Megan, get yourself a shovel.

Mrs Peel *rushes off.*

Mrs Peel   We're bein' overrun!

Megan *leaves without looking at* **James**. **Burns** *looks at* **Turner** *and* **Bug**.

Burns   Say we go finish the last a' that pie?

Burns *and* **James** *leave.*

Bug   Don't see why you're pissed at me.

Beat.

Bug   Aint nothin' I can do about it, Turn.

Turner   It's bullshit!

Bug   It just the way it goes. You know that.

Turner   Fuckin' sick a' it, s'what I know.

Bug   Aint like I'm not comin' back here.

Turner   When! A year? Two? Three –

Bug   Shit I don't know.

Turner   I do! I know that we got plans. I know that we can see them plans through. This. This here situation, don't ruin them plans if we don't let it. What it does is bring them plans closer. We been talkin' about doin' this thing later, fuck it, we do it now. We do it tonight. We camp out. We don't come back here.

Pause.

Bug   You talkin' about bein' an Illegal, Turn.

Turner   We aint gonna be Illegals.

Bug   S'what you sayin'.

Turner   S'fuckin' word that don't mean shit for us.

Bug   S'word that gets us struck off the register.

Turner   We don't need to be on it.

Bug   What a' you talkin' about?

Turner   We'd be self sufficient. We wouldn't need any a' their tinned hand outs. We'd be on our own and botherin' nobody. We wouldn't be livin' in a squalor terrace. We'd find a place in the middle a' nowhere, we know the drill Bug. We know where Security go and don't go –

Bug   We are Security!

Turner   I know what we are. And I know what we could be.

Beat.

Bug   I aint doin' it till we can do it right. I couldn't be alright with what I done over these years if I thought that given the chance I'd do same as them.

Turner   I aint the same as them!

Bug   I dint say that –

Turner   I fought in war after war –

Bug   I never said you dint.

Turner   You never said nothin'.

Turner *leaves.*

Scene Eight

Stables. Evening. Violent rain.

James *waits.* **Megan** *enters.*

James   Dint know if you were gonna come.

Megan   Just passin' by.

James   Been waitin here all night.

Megan   Washed my hair.

James   Haven't had a chance –

Megan   Don't want to talk about it.

Pause.

Megan   Mince hasn't been eatin'.

Beat.

James   Didn't know that.

Megan   Two days now.

James   Not like him.

Beat.

Megan   Chickens haven't laid eggs.

James   Had an egg this morning.

Megan   You had an old egg.

Beat.

James   Megan –

Megan   Don't want to talk about it.

Pause.

Megan   Dropped a plate this afternoon.

Beat.

James   It break?

Megan   Million pieces.

James   Megan stop –

Megan   Don't want to talk about it.

Beat.

Megan   Beans a' spoilt.

Beat.

Megan   A tree fell.

Beat.

Megan   Barn door's smashed.

Beat.

Megan   Cow's dead.

Beat.

Megan (*Cries.*)   Don't want to cry about it.

James *goes towards her but she steps back.*

Megan   Don't want to be left behind.

James   Don't want to leave.

Megan   Don't want to be alone.

James   I'm coming back.

James *moves closer to her.*

Megan   Don't want to wait.

James   Ssshh.

Megan   Don't want to want.

James   Ssshh.

Megan   Don't want to want you.

Beat.

Megan   Want you.

James   Want you too.

Megan   Want you to love me.

James   Already do.

Beat.

James   Love you.

Pause.

Megan   Love you.

Beat.

James   I love you.

Beat.

Megan (*Smiles.*)   I love you.

James (*Smiles.*)   I love you.

Megan (*Smiles.*)   I love you.

James (*Laughs.*)   I love you!

Megan (*Laughs.*)   I love you!

James (*Shouts.*)   I love you!

Megan   Ssshh. Want you to make love to me.

Blackout.

Act Two

Scene One

Kitchen. Noon. Violent rain.

Mrs Peel *and* **Megan** *are stacking and checking crates of vegetables.* **Burns** *enters jauntily, carrying a rifle and wet from rain.*

Burns   I just hung you up a fine young hind.

Mrs Peel   That don't mean pig pee to me right now Burns.

Burns *puts the rifle down, notices the crates.*

Mrs Peel   Barn roof fixin' up s'what I need.

Burns   It comin' in bad?

Mrs Peel   I've stopped counting how much I've lost to fungus.

Burns   Nothin' I can do about it in this rain.

Mrs Peel   He's got me by the balls this time.

Burns   Soon as it stops I'll get up there, see to it.

Mrs Peel   Should a' been seen to before now.

Burns   I done some a' it.

Mrs Peel   That been six week ago.

Burns   Few days work and it'll be finished. Never seen so many hares about. Must a' been a spike in 'em, bought back two a' them as well. Almost missed the hind, was takin' a piss when I seen it and just as I'm at the trigger somethin' must a' spooked it cause it bolted.

Mrs Peel (*Lowers her gaze.*)   Dint finish that job neither.

Burns *zips up his fly.* **Turner** *enters, wet and sulky.*

Turner   I aint campin' up the grit stone no more. Aint had a piss in two days, case I got fast there on the spot. Aint had a wash and I'm salty as a wet dog. Fuckin' stupid-cuntin' tent caved in on me twice. I had to wallop my boots inta that bastard horse's lungs to get it to budge. And I been on a saddle way to fuckin' hell and back. I aint campin' up the grit stone no more!

Beat.

Turner   Cup a' tea'd be nice.

Mrs Peel *puts the tea on*.

Burns   I was gonna ask for that nice hare and onion stew you made for us one time?

Mrs Peel   Aint makin' that again, makes you fart.

Burns   Only . . . Bug's gettin' back here today.

Mrs Peel   I definitely aint makin' no stew.

Megan *is devastated*.

Turner   You dint tell me that!

Burns   You just got in.

Turner   When's he comin'?

Burns   Tonight.

Turner   Shit. We aint ready. we done nothin' for him.

Burns   Be nice to make him that stew.

Mrs Peel   He gonna get what he get.

Megan   This must be a good sign.

Turner   He aint gonna want no stew.

Megan   Must mean they gonna send more back.

Turner   He gonna want lamb.

Mrs Peel   He aint gettin' it.

Megan   They say that, Burns?

Turner   We gotta get one a' them lambs on a spit.

Mrs Peel   I need them sheep for milk.

Turner   You don't need all a' 'em.

Mrs Peel   Sheep only got two teats, I need every teat I got!

Turner   I knowed he gonna come back. How the fuck he swing that?

Stands and raises his flask.

To that jammy fuckin' bastard.

Burns   To bringin' 'em home.

Megan *has finally got her answer.*

Megan   To bringin' 'em home.

Chink – they belt one back. **Megan** *and* **Turner** *are up and about the kitchen.*

Turner   We'll camp out early tonight.

Megan   We should all celebrate here.

Burns   Don't go throwin' that bag out, can get another cup out a' that.

Mrs Peel (*Dumps the tea bag.*)   I know how to make a cup a' tea.

Turner   Take some steaks out with us.

Megan   You could both stay here.

Burns   Now why'd you do that?

Mrs Peel   I made three cups out a' it.

Turner   We got some sides a' deer.

Megan   That way we could all hear about it.

Burns   I know, I was watchin'.

Mrs Peel   That bag had nothin' in it left to give.

Turner   We aint got enough whisky!

Burns   I think it has a little more life in it yet.

Mrs Peel   One bag can make up to three cups.

Burns   Looks like yer got yourself a challenge there, Mrs Peel, cause I can make four.

Mrs Peel   I can make ten if you want 'em weak as cat piss!

Burns   I can make four cups, strong as they come, with one bag.

Mrs Peel   You're a bare-faced liar, Burns.

Burns   (*Staring at her.*) Turner, get me a tea bag and four cups.

Mrs Peel   (*Staring at him.*) Make that two bags and seven cups.

Beat. Everyone turns to **Turner**.

Turner (*Disbelief.*)   What?

Turner *does it.*

Burns   Who's judgin'?

Mrs Peel   You choose.

Burns   Which one of youse knows a good cuppa?

Megan *shoots her hand into the air.*

Burns   Alright, Megan it is. Second thing. What's at stake here?

Mrs Peel   What d'you mean?

Burns   We're doin' prizes.

Mrs Peel   Prizes?

Megan   Prizes!

Mrs Peel   Alright. You first.

Burns   I'd like to have a dance.

Beat.

Mrs Peel   What d'you mean?

Burns   I'd like to dance.

Mrs Peel (*Indifferent.*)   Alright.

Burns   You and me.

Turner   What?

Mrs Peel   I aint dancin'.

Burns   Man can't dance alone.

Mrs Peel   I aint dancin' with you, Burns.

Megan   I will!

Burns   Thought you was gonna' win?

Beat.

Mrs Peel   Alright. Stakes it is. I want a' go out on them moors with yer and get a deer.

Burns   Alright.

Turner   What?

Burns (*To* **Megan**.)   Ready?

Megan *begins the tasting, starting with* **Mrs Peel***'s three cups.*

Megan   They all good.

Mrs Peel *sniffs with pride and* **Megan** *moves on to* **Burns***'s cups.* **Megan** *maximizes her time as the centre of attention – she sips, slurps, ponders and gurgles.*

Megan   They all good!

Mrs Peel   You win.

Turner *pats* **Burns** *on the back,* **Megan** *claps,* **Mrs Peel** *smiles.* **Bug** *enters, his left arm is now a stump.*

Turner   You're early.

Bug *drops his bag down.*

Turner   Nothin's ready.

Bug   S'alright.

Megan *looks as if she might burst into tears, she leaves.*

Burns (*Shakes his hand.*)   Good to have yer back.

Bug   Good to be back.

Turner   Where the fuck you been?

Turner *slings his arms around* **Bug**, *they wrestle and laugh.* **Mrs Peel** *leaves.*

Turner   Fuckin' leavin' me.

Burns   Let's have a drink.

They belt one back.

Turner (*Nods to the stump.*)   So, what happened there then?

Bug   Lost it.

Turner It give yer any trouble?

Bug   Can hurt. Just adaptin' to it.

Turner Least you can still pull your prick.

Burns   How's Brian?

Bug   We were nowhere near his regiment.

Burns   What? But you were south.

Bug   Couldn't get no word to him.

Turner   How's James?

Burns   You get my letter to him?

Bug   I'm sorry, Burns.

Turner   He doin' us proud?

Burns   A they bringin' any a' 'em back?

Bug   There are soldiers . . . there are soldiers . . .

Beat. **Burns** *sits down.*

Turner   Want somethin' to eat?

Bug   I'm alright with this.

Turner   What'd they drink over there?

Bug   Rum.

Turner   S'alright.

Bug   Yeah. Prefer whiskey.

Turner   We aint got much a' it.

Bug   They shippin' less over?

Turner   Halved our supplies, s'only thing we get short a'. Way we set up here now, we eatin' none a' that tinned shit. It gonna be steak and taters we puttin' on the fire tonight. Times we back here we gettin' meat and two veg, stews with mash . . . all kinds a' shit. And then there's breakfast. Full on fried breakfast!

Bug   Sounds good. So what's been goin' on?

Turner   Jack shit been happenin' out here.

Bug   Not many Illegals?

Turner   We aint been gettin' many. Its impossible to do the job, just the two a' us out there. (*Chinks Bug's flask.*) But that's all set to change now eh?

Bug   What about outside?

Turner (*Shrugs.*)   Government set up a lottery for them that want kids.

Bug   They lifted the ban?

Turner   S'lottery, Bug.

Bug   Right.

Turner   One in ten thousand. How long it take to get back?

Bug   What about China?

Turner (*Shrugs*.)   What about it?

Bug   Allies declared war two week ago.

Turner   Aint affectin' us, none a' our troops a' bein' deployed.

Bug   It a different war they startin' over there.

Turner   How long it take to get back?

Bug   Near on three days.

Turner   Shit.

Bug   Yeah. Tried to get a few winks on the train up there.

Turner   Too worried for that, I bet.

Bug   Well . . . I'm gonna go crash for a couple a' hours.

Turner   Now?

Bug *nods.*

Turner   You just got here.

Bug   I'm tired, Turn.

Turner   Alright.

Bug *goes back to his bag.*

Bug   Bought you a piece a' kit back.

Turner   Arh, yes! It some a' their kit?

Bug   Yeah.

Turner   Vest? Pair a' eyes?

Bug   Aint nothin' like that. It a radio.

Bug *gives the radio to* **Burns**.

Burns (*Nods.*)   Good to have yer back.

Turner   I'll come and get yer in a couple a' hours.

Bug *nods and leaves*.

Turner   Why the fuck dint you tell me he'd got a stump?

Burns   I dint know.

Turner   Must a' looked like a right cunt, dint know what to say.

Burns   Coulda fooled me, pullin' his prick.

Turner   I can't treat him like he's disabled. It's Bug, same old, arm or no arm. And anyway, that's what yer supposed to do . . . acknowledge it.

Beat.

Can you ride a horse with a stump?

Burns *shrugs, drinks*.

Burns   Now we know how come he's back.

Turner   Yeah.

Burns   Never seen him like that.

Turner   Tired, s'all.

Burns   More than that.

Turner   Couple a' hours sleep he'll be right.

Burns   Seen it in his eyes.

Burns *leaves with the radio*.

Turner   He gonna be fine.

Scene Two

Stables. Evening.

Megan *is sat, she has been crying.* **Turner** *enters stealthily.*

Megan (*Spins round.*)   You scared me!

Turner   Whooah. You been cryin'?

Megan   No.

Turner   Looks to me like you have.

Megan   Haven't.

Turner (*Offers her a fag.*)   Fag? You sure?

Megan   Don't smoke.

Turner   Since when?

Megan   Never liked 'em much.

Turner   Used to smoke a lot a' mine to say you din't like 'em.

Beat.

Turner   Want a' talk about it?

Megan   Nothin' a' talk about.

Turner   Might help if you did. I'll take a guess. You seen what happened to Bug and you worried about James.

Megan   Why would I be worried about him?

Turner   I seen him headin' over here at night, Megan. And I knowed you in here too. I dint say nothin' to you about it. Just accepted it I guess. Don't mean that I stopped . . . shit, you know . . . carin' about you.

Megan *looks at* **Turner**.

Turner   S'how you holdin' up?

Megan   Miss him. Miss him a lot.

Turner   Yeah. I bet he's missin' you too. Who wouldn't? You're quite a girl Megan. I'll tell you somethin' from experience. When a man's been with you it's pretty hard to come back from that. Yeah. You really set the standard for me. Raised the bar. And in all sorts a' ways, not just . . . (*Laughs with embarrassment.*) You know. Shit. I aint no good at this. I just wanted to see you were alright. I'm gonna' go. Leave you to it.

Turner *walks away.*

Megan   Stay.

Turner   Well, alright.

Megan   We could talk.

Turner   I'd like that.

Beat.

Megan   Bird flew inta the kitchen window yesterday.

Turner   Yeah?

Megan   I was right there in front a' it washin' the dishes when it hit the glass. Made a big thuddin' sound, scared me. Then it flew off. But it left somethin' behind. A white powder in the shape a' it wings. Like a ghost a' it. I been lookin' at that all day and no one seen it, not even Mrs Peel. I dint tell her, case she rubbed it away.

Turner   I'll have to take a look at that.

Megan   Won't be there no more cause a' the rain.

Turner   Some things just don't last long enough, do they?

Beat.

Megan   Never knowed you cared about me.

Turner   I'm no good at sayin' stuff like that.

Megan   That mean you'd look out for me?

Turner   I done it before, remember.

Beat.

You were gonna be sent away.

Megan   I know.

Turner   Don't seem like it.

Megan   You told me. But it different now.

Turner   It sure is. S'like you been avoidin' me.

Megan   You'd help me if . . . if I needed it?

Turner   You know I would.

Megan   James would too.

Turner   But he aint here.

Megan   He gonna come back. Just don't know when.

Turner *takes out his flask politely offers* **Megan** *a drink.*

Megan   I shouldn't.

Turner   Why?

Megan   It too early for that.

Turner   Have a slug anyway, for old time's sake.

Megan *drinks; spills some down her chin.*

Turner   Looks like you forgotten how to handle your drink.

They both laugh; she gives him back the flask.

Turner   Come on, you can do better than that.

Megan *shakes her head.* **Turner** *insists.* **Megan** *has another drink.*

Turner   S'like old times. We did have us some good times together. You remember that time when you, me and Bug been up all night drinkin'? You were drinkin' like a fish, couldn't get enough a' the stuff.

Megan   I got work to do now.

Turner   Laughin' and smilin' you were.

Megan *tries to pass but* **Turner** *blocks her way.*

Turner   You do have a lovely smile. Really lights up a room, lights up . . . (*Smiles.*) Anyway, so there we all are with an empty bottle on the table between us. Not a drop left. And you . . . (*Laughs.*)

Megan   Don't!

Turner   You took hold a' the bottle.

Megan   Please don't.

Turner   And let us both have a go. Didn't you? What's this . . . tears? No, no, you don't understand. I dint tell James about it. I wouldn't do that. I wouldn't spoil what you got goin' there. Cause, it would. Wouldn't it? I mean, if he knew that what sweet Megan here likes (*shakes his head and laughs to himself.*) and I mean really likes is bein' fucked dirty. He would feel insecure about that. Cause he didn't fuck you like that. Did he? (*Sympathetically.*) I dint think so.

Megan   Leave mc alone.

Turner   I wish I could, but when you look at me with those sad eyes a' yours, s'like lookin' at a deer before I slam it down to the ground. Gets me hard.

Turner *takes off his jacket,* **Megan** *edges backwards.*

Turner   See, all's I want is to throw you a nice, hard fuck. Yeah, that's right. (*Edges forwards.*) All's I want is to take that nice long hair a' yours and use it like a pair a' reigns. (*Grabs* **Megan***'s hair.*) Alls I want is to saddle up and –

The horses whinny. **Burns** *enters.*

Burns   What's goin' on here!

Turner *releases* **Megan***.*

Turner   Nothin'.

Burns   I don't give a flyin' fuck that you out here in the wilderness, you wanna' shove that dick a' yours in somethin' I suggest you start takin' a likin' to livestock. That understood?

Turner *nods.* **Burns** *steps aside.* **Turner** *leaves.*

Burns   He bother you again, you come to me about it.

Burns *makes to leave.*

Megan   It a good sign, Bug comin' back?

Burns   You seen his arm.

Megan   He came back alive.

Burns   They don't bring the dead back.

Beat.

Burns   Been waitin' three years for my boy to come back. You can't keep waitin'.

Burns *leaves.* **Megan** *drops to her knees and cries. The horses whinny.* **James**, *dressed in civvies, enters.* **Megan** *slowly stands to her feet and looks at* **James** *for a few seconds. She smiles and he smiles back at her. She laughs and he laughs. She slowly walks towards him, the distant sound of gunfire and explosions are heard, until they are stood opposite one another.*

James   It a gift.

James *edges backwards away from* **Megan** *as the sound of gunfire and explosions become louder and call him back, until he finally disappears.*

Scene Three

Peak. Late afternoon. **Bug** *and* **Turner** *are sat quietly drinking.*

Bug   Missed this quiet.

Turner   Like it too, but shit I had enough a' it these past months.

Bug   Been on your own out here?

Turner   Pretty much. Wind, hoof beats . . . caw of a bird, that been it for me.

Bug   My ears a' still ringing.

Turner   Get laid much.

Bug   Wasn't like that.

Turner (*Shakes his flask.*)   Shit, this aint gonna last us two days.

Bug   Way you been going at it, it aint gonna get us through tonight.

Turner   We need to take this situation in hand.

Bug   What d'you mean?

Turner   Taters make vodka, right?

Bug   Yeah, but, you need somethin' else too.

Turner   What?

Bug   Alcohol I guess.

Turner *and* **Bug** *laugh a little*.

Turner   S'what I missed the most, talkin' shit to somebody. There been times out here when the drag of a cloud been the biggest event a' my day. Don't know how I've done it. (*Drinks.*) But it given me the time to figure a' few things, like I said was gonna . . . about that place a' ours. Not that cock-eyed-bullshit I been spoutin' before you left. (*Half laughs.*) The shit I been spewin'. I can be a crazy bastard sometimes, I know that. But you should a' just laid one on me. Had it a' been the other way round I'd a done it to you. I don't mean that. It'll be when it'll be. But. Just how you seen it that first time I told it, I seen it too.

Bug   Turn . . .

Turner   I aint shittin' you. There been times up on that
saddle, when I seen it right there on the horizon. Perched
on its own, nothin' but weather around it. I'd keep on its
trail, laughin' at myself some, knowin' it aint there . . . but
the horse'd pick it up a little, like it felt the pull a' it too. It'd
still be some fifty mile a' so ahead a' me, when I'd start to see
them stones it made up a', solid granite, every one a' 'em . . .
pokey windows that don't let much light in. After a while I'd
throw my eyeline away and when I looked back it wouldn't
be there no more . . . but soon as the sun dropped, I'd see an
orange glut a' flame from the fireplace. There'd be steak and
taters on it, pile a' cards at the ready . . .

Beat.

Turner   S'gonna be lot a' fuckin' work too. Aint gonna be
how I'm tellin' it now when we get hold a' it. But way I see it
every inch a' fencin' we put up, every plank a' wood we sand,
every blister on our backs, be worth it cause it's for us. Our
own fuckin' thing.

Beat.

Bug   Been thinkin' I'd a' liked to a' been married again.

Turner (*Laughs.*)   Married?

Bug   Yeah.

Turner (*Stops laughing.*)   You never told me you been
married.

Bug   Me and her been eighteen, had ourselves the biggest
weddin'. Three white limos, nine bridesmaids, three page
boys, hundred and forty eight guests, seven tier wedding
cake, and a mountain a' profiteroles with a six foot chocolate
fountain for them that dint like icin' or dried fruit. She left
me after three months to start up with the weddin'
photographer. He said he could get her modellin' career
goin' . . . We'd a' had a baby we'd a' been alright.

Turner   Best thing you did gettin' rid a' her.

Bug   We been arguin' most a the time, dint laugh twice.

Turner   That's it, birds aren't funny.

Bug   Some birds a' funny.

Turner   Name one bird we know who's funny?

Bug   We don't know any birds . . . Mrs Peel got a sense a' humour.

Turner   She got a crusty fanny as well. Dint think about the wives.

Bug   Just sayin' it's somethin' I'd a' liked to a done before now.

Beat.

Bug   Shouldn't think about gettin' that place, Turn.

Turner   Why's that?

Bug   Can't see it no more.

Turner   Yeah? Well I can.

Bug   Don't see us here much longer.

Turner   What a' you talkin' about?

Bug   Need all the men they got.

Turner   Need men back here too.

Bug   Somethin's gotta give.

Turner   Security's weak as it is.

Bug   Bulk a' the army aint enough.

Turner   Fuck it I'll go and come back.

Bug   There aint no comin' back.

Turner   What a' you fuckin' sayin'?

Bug   They aint comin' back.

Turner   You fuckin' did.

Bug   Set the grenade off myself.

Pause.

Turner   Had our backs to the wall plenty a' times.

Bug   Aint like what it been before.

Turner   I know what it's fuckin' like.

Bug   No you don't.

Turner   I fuckin' do!

Bug   There aint no talkin' to you sometimes.

Turner   Not when you're talkin' shit.

Bug   You don't wanna' hear it.

Turner   There aint nothin' you can tell me.

Turner *turns around.* **Bug** *stays as he is.*

Turner   You're just pissed about your arm.

Bug   You dint hear what I said.

Turner   I fuckin' heard yer. I don't believe yer.

Turner *is striding aimlessly behind* **Bug**.

Turner   You . . . you couldn't a' done that. You hear! You dint do that . . . leave me waitin' out here . . . weren't gonna do that . . . couldn't a' left me out here . . . You wanna drop me? S'that what you fuckin' want? Need to take that stump out on someone? Go ahead. I can take it. Come on. Lay one on me. Fuckin' turn around. Fuckin' come on and get it. (*Draws back a blow.*) I'll fuck you –

A fighter jet screeches overhead. **Turner** *hits the ground,* **Bug** *doesn't react.*

Turner   Shit! Shit shit shit did you hear that? (*Laughs.*) We got jets. (*On his knees.*) We . . . we got jets.(*On his feet.*) We got jets in the sky! Woo-Hoo!

Bug   Aint ours.

Beat.

Turner   What?

Bug   Jets, aint ours.

Turner   What d'you mean?

Bug   Our allies set up an airbase outside a' Sheffield.

Turner   What a' they doin' here?

Bug   Firin' misiles.

Turner   Where to?

Bug   China. Turn, they been –

Turner   Still, good to see somethin' up there.

Turner *stares at* **Bug** *defiantly. Pause.* **Bug** *walks away.*

Bug   Goin' back to the outpost tomorrow.

Turner   We out here for two days.

Another fighter jet screeches overhead. Turner runs after it, making whooping noises.

Scene Four

Plot of land. Sunset.

Mrs Peel *is harvesting potatoes from the earth.* **Burns** *enters, he has been drinking heavily but wears it well. He stands at a distance to her looking out.*

Burns   Quite a sunset.

Beat.

Burns   More orange than usual. Don't yer think?

Mrs Peel   Aint lookin' at it.

Burns   Late in the day to be doin' that.

Burns *edges closer to* **Mrs Peel**.

Burns   That was a fine dinner.

Mrs Peel   Not keen on snails.

Burns   Don't like the taste or the look a' 'em?

Mrs Peel   Just don't fancy 'em after lookin' at 'em shit all day.

Burns   I been meanin' to ask what yer put with 'em?

Mrs Peel   Garlic and sage. Same as I do everythin'.

Burns   Used to do a bit a' cookin' myself.

Mrs Peel   Let me know if you should get the urge again.

Burns   I wouldn't be able to do what you do.

Mrs Peel   I'm out a' whiskey.

Burns   Got some here.

Burns *gives his flask to* **Mrs Peel**.

Burns   I'm gettin' supplies in the mornin'.

Mrs Peel *gives the flask back*.

Burns   Put you a bottle under the sink.

Mrs Peel *doesn't acknowledge the bottle; continues working*.

Burns   What a' you cookin' for dinner tomorrow?

Mrs Peel   Snails.

Burns   Again?

Mrs Peel   Had to put some a' em aside. They weren't shittin'.

Burns   Constipated snails?

Mrs Peel   And mashed tater.

Burns   Been thinkin' about makin' some changes around here.

Mrs Peel   What kind a' changes?

Burns   Not now.

Mrs Peel *stands*.

Mrs Peel   What kind a changes?

Burns   A greenhouse.

The potato falls away from **Mrs Peel***'s hand.*

Burns   Build a greenhouse so as we can get more fruit. Fix the roofin' a' the stables. Make a stone oven for outside. Take some cuttin's and plant some flowers. Get some beehives. Four, five beehives for honey and . . . what's that other stuff called yer get from 'em?

Mrs Peel   Royal jelly.

Burns   Yeah, royal jelly. What d'yer say?

Mrs Peel (*Becomes* **Mrs Peel**.)   More work. But. Alright.

Beat.

Burns   How come in all this time I never known your first name?

Mrs Peel   Cause I never told yer, Burns.

Burns   It's Keith . . . Keith. Is it out a' respect for a Mr Peel?

Mrs Peel   Are you drunk!

Burns   No.

Mrs Peel (*Crouches down.*)   Then stop talkin' shit.

Mrs Peel *shoves potatoes into the sack,* **Burns** *crouches down before her.*

Burns (*Takes the sack.*)   Why ruin what we got here?

Mrs Peel (*Grabs the sack back.*)   We aint got nothin'.

Burns   But we could have.

Burns *swoops* **Mrs Peel** *onto her back and arches over her like a dog.*

Mrs Peel   Bleedin' 'ell fire and Jack!

Burns   Mrs Peel you got enough balls for ten men, can drink any man under the table, give a man as good as yer get, swear like a trooper, work harder than most a' the men I know. And yet! You've got the bosom of a Goddess. (*Bends forwards.*) The carriage of an eagle. And I bet your packin' as much heat in that cave a' yours as the earth's core. (*Bends forwards.*) That bein' with you would be a *hot* and *molten* –

Mrs Peel *slaps* **Burns**'*s face.*

Burns (*Strokes his cheek.*)   How about you and me take a moonlight swim?

Mrs Peel   I could choke you.

Mrs Peel *bolts to her feet and* **Burns** *chases after her.*

Mrs Peel   You wanna' keep that dead squid a' yours away from me!

Burns   I can assure you it's *alive!*

Mrs Peel *grabs a shovel and threatens to clobber* **Burns** *with it.*

Mrs Peel   It won't be if you come any closer.

Burns   Why don't you and me step inside and get to it?

Mrs Peel   I'd rather be under a rabid dog.

Burns   How about we just drop the lip on?

Mrs Peel   I'd rather be sat on the shitter with diarrhoea and toothache.

Burns   We could have ourselves a cuddle?

Mrs Peel   I'd rather . . . I got a tough enough life as it is without stavin' off the advances of a sex maniac! (*From the gut.*) Now step away!

Burns *does.*

Mrs Peel   I don't know who you think you're playin' with.

Burns   I aint playin'.

Mrs Peel *walks away.*

Burns   I'm sweet on you!

Beat.

Burns   How about you and me go get your deer?

Mrs Peel *stops.*

Burns   Tomorrow?

Beat.

Burns   That a date?

Beat.

Mrs Peel   I guess.

Mrs Peel *leaves.*

Scene Five

Kitchen. Morning.

Megan *is folding a pile of washed and dried clothes and sheets.*
Bug *enters.*

Bug   I been needin' to talk to you too.

Megan   Me?

Beat.

Megan   Why?

Beat. **Megan** *sees it in* **Bug**'s *eyes. She grabs a sheet from the pile.*

Megan   Give me a hand foldin' these sheets?

Bug *looks at his stump.*

Megan   We'll just fold it best we can.

Bug   Can we sit down?

Megan   They so big we got a' stand and do it.

Megan *gives some of the sheet to* **Bug** *to hold on to.*

Megan   You keep hold a' this here.

Bug   I need to tell you somethin'.

Megan *steps away from* **Bug**.

Megan   I can hear you from here.

Megan *takes the corners and opens the stained sheet out.*

Megan   Don't know how these stains got here.

Megan *halves the width of the sheet.*

Bug   Its James.

Megan *halves the width of the sheet again.*

Megan   I think it Burns.

Megan *halves the width of the sheet again.*

Megan   He drink so much he must a' been sick on 'em.

Megan *walks towards* **Bug** *and takes the sheet off him.*

Bug   He's dead.

Megan *halves the length of the sheet.*

Megan   It gonna kill him one day.

Megan *halves the length of the sheet again.*

Bug   Dint have no pain.

Megan *halves the length of the sheet again.*

Megan   Bet his liver do.

Megan *folds the sheet, folds it again and again.*

Bug   He talked about you –

Megan   Don't.

Beat.

Megan   Don't say no more.

Bug *leaves.* **Megan** *holds the tightly folded sheet to her chest as if it were the dead's flag.* **Mrs Peel** *enters, eyes* **Megan** *shaking from behind.*

Mrs Peel   You holdin' yourself again?

Megan *nods slowly.* **Mrs Peel** *shakes her head, sights the rest of the garments.*

Mrs Peel   Fold the rest a' them things.

Megan *leaves with the sheet.*

Mrs Peel   You come back here.

Mrs Peel *storms after* **Megan** *but stops dead in her tracks as* **Burns** *enters, holding the radio.*

Mrs Peel (*Gruff.*)   What d'you want?

Mrs Peel *looks away from* **Burns**; *he stays where he is.*

Mrs Peel   We goin' after my deer?

Mrs Peel *looks at* **Burns**.

Mrs Peel   Where's the supplies?

Mrs Peel *looks searchingly at* **Burns**.

Mrs Peel   Burns?

Burns *turns up the volume, beautiful music plays, and puts the radio down.*

Burns (*softly*)   I want my dance.

Mrs Peel (*Relieved but stern.*)   I aint dancin'.

Burns *walks towards* **Mrs Peel**.

Mrs Peel   Are you outta your mind! I aint dancin' in here! I got work to do! I never said when!

Burns *stands still before* **Mrs Peel**.

Burns   We only got now.

Burns *takes* **Mrs Peel**'s *hand. They dance; he is surprisingly light on his toes whilst she is as stiff as a fence post. He looks at her whilst she looks away. Gradually their steps become smaller and smaller until they are stood still.* **Burns** *looks at* **Mrs Peel** *for what feels like a long time but is only a moment, she looks back at him. They lean very slowly towards one another.*

Turner (*Offstage.*)   Why'd you leave without me?

Bug (*Offstage.*)   Told you I was comin' back.

Mrs Peel *jolts away from* **Burns** *and darts over to the radio.* **Mrs Peel** *tunes the radio as* **Turner** *and* **Bug** *walk in.*

Turner   You could a' woke me up.

Bug   Thought you were stayin' on.

Turner   Well I thought both a' us were.

Mrs Peel   Quiet!

Radio (*American.*)   . . . resulting in the disarmament of the airbase and the withdrawal of the British Security from the Sheffield area which took place at ten hundred hours GMT. Plans today were revealed for a monument to commemorate the fallen dead in China.

Turner   Withdrawal?

Beat.

Turner   What's the disarmament of the airbase got to do with us?

Beat.

Turner   What the fuck does . . . withdrawal mean?

Burns   Means we aint there no more.

Turner   But . . . if we aint there then who is?

Beat.

Who's controllin' Sheffield?

Beat.

Turner   No, no, they . . . they bein' quarantined. S'why we pulled out. Fuck, I don't know, there enough diseases. (*To* **Mrs Peel**.) Put our radio on.

Burns   It's dead.

Turner   What d'you mean?

Turner *goes to the radio . . . it's dead.*

Turner   You gonna tell me what the fuck's going on?

Burns   I put it on this mornin' at around five and it was dead. I left for the station cause I had to pick up the supplies and the freight never showed.

Turner   What? Why? Station ain't even in Sheffield.

Burns   What did you hear in the beginnin'?

Mrs Peel   Ultimatum expired.

Turner   What ultimatum?

Mrs Peel   Dint hear no more.

Turner   I'm . . . I'm . . . I don't know what's goin' on.

Burns   Civilians gave an ultimatum?

Turner   We gave one to them? We gave 'em an ultimatum, right?

Burns   We the ones who've withdrawn.

Turner   We don't know what that means.

Burns   Means we pulled –

Turner   I know that! We don't know why.

Mrs Peel   Why's it been broadcast over there?

Turner   Cause a' the airbase, it's theirs.

Mrs Peel   Why a' they here?

Turner   They're not anymore. Security gonna be headin' over there.

Burns   Maybe civilians a' headin' out there.

Turner   The Sheffield border'll still be there.

Burns   Said withdrew from the area. Area? Area? That aint specific.

Beat.

Burns   We ride out, see what's goin' on.

Mrs Peel   Aint it better to wait here?

Burns If they comin', no.

Turner They aint comin' out here, there gonna be Security from all over.

Burns (*To* **Mrs Peel**.)   We'll go to a settlement, ask there.

Turner (*To* **Bug**.) You comin'?

Burns   You stay here till we get back.

Turner *leaves.* **Burns** *and* **Mrs Peel** *look at each other, at* **Bug** *stood in the distance between them, then back at each other.*

Burns   I'll be goin' then.

Burns *makes to leave.*

Mrs Peel   How long you gonna be?

Burns   Few hours.

They look at **Bug** *(oblivious that he is an obstacle) and then at the floor.*

Mrs Peel   How many?

Burns   Four.

Mrs Peel   Four?

Burns   Five, maybe.

They look at each other.

Burns   Can't say for sure.

Mrs Peel   No, course not.

Burns *makes to leave; stops.*

Burns   About yesterday . . .

Mrs Peel *looks at* **Bug**.

Mrs Peel   What about it?

Burns   The way I . . .

Burns *looks at* **Bug**.

Burns   Don't want yer to think that I just wanted . . .

They both look at **Bug**, *then at each other.*

Burns   I could sit and listen to you say the alphabet.

Beat.

Turner (*Offstage.*)   Burns!

Burns   I gotta go now.

Burns *leaves.* **Mrs Peel** *stands still for a few seconds; feels his absence. She starts folding the washing that* **Megan** *left behind. The rain continues to pour.*

Bug   You remember the drizzle, Mrs Peel?

Beat.

Bug   Constant . . . steady. Never seemed to end, did it? People complained about that. But it dint really affect us much. We were used to it. But now, it's different. Violent . . . unpredictable. I been out in the worst a' it. Laid there at night listenin' to it. Thinkin' to myself this can't go on . . . and it always did. But now . . . I think the atmosphere's finally broken apart.

Mrs Peel *has stopped folding.*

Bug   You understand what I mean?

Beat.

Mrs Peel   I was out walkin' one time just after a downpour a' rain. The kind we weren't used to back then. I'm walkin' close to a stream and further down on a rock I see a deer. Mindin' its own business, grazin' it was. When out a' nowhere, and at a deadly speed, a ragin' current a' water is comin' right at it. Deer freezes as the water rises all around it. Before, life was like a meanderin' stream. Takin' its time. Movin' casually. Now, it's like a flash flood. Deceptive. Can get you anytime.

Mrs Peel *picks up the pile of washing.*

Bug   What the deer do?

Mrs Peel   It got the fuck out a' there.

Mrs Peel *leaves.*

Bug   Too late.

Scene Six

Kitchen. Afternoon. Four hours have passed. Rain.

Megan *is sat peeling potatoes.* **Mrs Peel** *is tuning the American radio – various scraps of news, weather, music – she switches it off. She goes to the window, stares out for a while. She comes away from the window and sits at the table. Pause.*

Mrs Peel   Takin' too much skin off.

Mrs Peel *fiddles with the potato peelings.*

Mrs Peel   Look at that, waste a' tater. (*Suddenly alert.*)
That horses?

Mrs Peel *rushes to the window.*

Mrs Peel   Wind . . . just hearing the wind.

Mrs Peel *comes away from the window.*

Mrs Peel   I need to get that bird in the oven, it's as old as
me and it'll end up as tough if I don't have it in long enough.
You muckin' out them stables after that. Mulch some a' the
shit inta soil. Then yer can give me a hand gettin' them
sheep inta the byres . . . winter's on its way in . . . gotta pluck
that bird . . . I'll peel them taters.

Mrs Peel *goes to* **Megan**.

Mrs Peel   Give me the knife.

Megan   I know how to peel a' tater.

Mrs Peel   You abusin' that tater.

Megan *lobs the tater.*

Megan   That's abuse.

Beat.

Mrs Peel   Pick it up.

Megan   You pick it up.

Mrs Peel   I dint throw it.

Megan   You thrown away everythin' else.

Mrs Peel   Watch your mouth.

Megan   Say what I want.

Mrs Peel   Not to me you won't.

Megan   You don't want a' hear it.

Mrs Peel   Damn right I don't.

Megan   None a' you did, none a' you ever did, all this is cause a' you.

Mrs Peel   You have no right –

Megan   I have my right cause you had everythin' and left me nothin'.

Mrs Peel   We're all payin' for it.

Megan   You made your bed and you lyin' in it.

Mrs Peel   How dare you.

Megan   You been told / you been warned.

Mrs Peel   I marched! I protested!

Megan   You knew what would happen.

Mrs Peel   We dint know it would be like –

Megan (*Screams.*)   You let it get to this! You let the sea rise and flooded cities, burst river banks and destroyed our houses. You used up oil, made cars stop, forced us inta towns. You made us share rooms, put us in factories, fed us rations, let us get sick. You let my brother die a' TB, made my mum hang herself, sent James to war . . . for a pipe . . . and you killed him . . .

Mrs Peel (*Shouts.*)   That's enough!

Megan (*Cries hideously.*)   You killed him.

Mrs Peel   Enough.

Megan (*Wails.*)   I have a baby.

(*Silence.*)

Mrs Peel   You stupid. Stupid. Stupid girl!

Pause.

Mrs Peel   How far gone?

Megan   Five months.

Mrs Peel   You tell me this now?

Megan   Dint want to get rid a' it.

Mrs Peel   You can't keep the damn thing!

Megan   It my baby.

Mrs Peel   You don't have that choice.

Megan   Made my choice.

Mrs Peel   You took that rod out?

Megan   It a gift.

Mrs Peel   No, no. You'll pay a price for it.

Turner, *blood on his clothes, enters.*

Mrs Peel   Where's Burns?

Turner   Where's Bug?

Mrs Peel (*Quietly.*)   Where's Burns?

Turner   Need to tell Bug . . . there's too many a' 'em . . . they, they comin' from everywhere . . . runnin' right past us like we aint even there . . . like we nothin' . . . like we aint what they afraid a' . . . where's Bug? Cause Burns . . . Burns is off his horse runnin' among 'em askin' . . . askin' why they runnin' . . . bullet come out a' nowhere . . . where's Bug? Need to tell him Burns's dead . . . that we gotta get out a' here cause . . . we been left. We been left behind. A train took all Security North this mornin' and no one thought to come the fuck out here and fuckin' tell us! (*Rage.*) Where's Bug?

Mrs Peel (*To* **Megan**.)   Wait outside.

Turner (*Rage.*)   They fuckin' left us out here to burn!

Turner *wheels round erratically.*

Mrs Peel (*To* **Megan**.)   Now.

Turner   Where's Bug?

Megan *leaves.*

Mrs Peel   He aint here.

Turner *is still frantic when suddenly he stands still, calm.*

Turner   I'm dyin' for some breakfast.

Beat.

Mrs Peel   I make it way past seven.

Turner *laughs a little.*

Turner   Yeah, guess it is.

Turner *walks away, stops, his back to* **Mrs Peel.**

Turner   They been firin' nuclear missiles from the airbase. Ultimatum expired. We're gettin' one back.

Turner *walks away,* **Mrs Peel** *goes after him.*

Mrs Peel   What d'you mean?

Turner *turns to* **Mrs Peel**.

Turner   Boom.

Turner *leaves.* **Mrs Peel** *steps backwards and sits in the chair where* **Megan** *sat before. She sits very still for a few seconds, then picks up a potato and peels it.* **Megan** *enters; watches* **Mrs Peel** *attempting to peel the potato with trembling hands. Pause.*

Mrs Peel *continues to peel the potato.*

Megan   It a good sign?

Mrs Peel *continues to peel the potato.*

Megan   Mrs Peel?

Mrs Peel *continues to peel.*

Megan   They risen like Burns said?

Mrs Peel *stops peeling.*

Megan   That what it mean?

Mrs Peel *looks at* **Megan**. *Pause.*

Mrs Peel   Yeah. Yeah. It do.

Megan   What that mean for us?

Mrs Peel   We'll soon find out.

Mrs Peel *wanders away.*

Megan   Where you goin'?

Mrs Peel   Make us a tea.

Scene Seven

Peak. Late afternoon.

Bug *is sat, holding his flask.* **Turner** *is stood.*

Turner   We gotta get up North.

Turner *looks at* **Bug** *who stares out vacantly.*

Turner   We got a' head up the Pennine Way.

Beat.

Turner   You hear what I said?

Beat.

Turner (*Kicks the flask.*)   Answer me you useless piece a' shit!

Beat. **Turner** *stiffens.*

Turner   Get up.

Beat.

Turner   Get up now.

Beat.

Turner   Get up we're goin'.

Beat.

Turner   Up. (*Kicks* **Bug***'s foot.*) Now.

Turner *walks away, stops, back turned to* **Bug**.

Turner   Get up!

Turner *puts his hands on his hips.*

Turner   On your feet soldier.

Bug   There are soldiers runnin' blind through smoke as another bomb slams down.

Turner (*Barks.*)   On your feet soldier.

Bug   Some are fallin', some are dragged down by the man behind.

Turner   On your fuckin' feet!

Bug   The earth buries 'em there and then together as the explosion ploughs the earth.

Turner (*Screams.*)   That's an order!

Bug   There are soldiers waitin' for order to retreat.

Turner (*Despair.*)   That's an order.

Bug   There are soldiers tryin' to sleep where they are cause the order never comes.

Turner (*Breaking.*)   I order you.

Bug   Explosions gun fire cries.

Turner (*Begging.*)   I order you under the authority of the Security to your feet.

Bug   Just have to stay where they are.

Turner *turns to* **Bug**.

Turner   I order you under the authority of this government to your feet.

Beat.

Bug   I no longer recognize this government.

Turner *leaves.*

Bug   There's a man. Young. Never seen him before. There are men runnin' fallin' cryin' all around him. He's on his knees. Can't take my eyes off a' him. The earth ploughs up around him. None a' it seems to matter. He's waitin' there on his knees. Then the sudden shock a' it. Couple a' instinctive jerkin' movements before bein' covered in earth.

Bug *kneels, slowly hangs his head, waits.*

Scene Eight

Plot of land. Late afternoon, the light is fading fast.

Mrs Peel *enters holding a bag of seeds,* **Megan** *is with her.*

Megan   Why a' we leavin'?

Mrs Peel   No need for us to be here no more, is there?

Megan *shakes her head.*

Megan   Don't seem real.

Mrs Peel   It'll sink in soon enough.

Mrs Peel *starts sowing seeds.*

Megan   There been a time when you and me were out here workin', and you spotted a hare munchin' away at your salad leaves. You snuck up behind and grabbed hold a' it. I followed you inta the kitchen and you dropped a blow on its neck. Hare froze as straight as a fence post. You held it whilst I pulled back the skin, and you must a' been hungry cause you chopped it up right there and then on the board inta chunks. I couldn't stop lookin' at them chunks cause they were movin'. Jitterin', like they were cold or somethin'. You put them chunks inta the pan and they still jitterin'. You put the heat on 'em and I say to you: them chunks are still alive! You say: they dead they just don't know it yet.

Beat.

Megan   I feel like I'm alive and I just don't know it yet.

Megan *turns to* **Mrs Peel**, *she looks away.*

Mrs Peel   Let's sow these seeds before it gets dark.

Mrs Peel *kneels down and sows.*

Megan   Why a' you sowin' seeds?

Mrs Peel   For the future.

Megan   But we aint gonna be here. Who gonna tend to it?

Mrs Peel   This soil don't need us. Everythin' that happens upon it – failure a' crops, spreadin' a diseases, flood, drought – don't mean nothin' to it. Only the sun matters. Where there's light there will be life. S'long as the sunrises all will be.

Megan   You should a' said that a long time ago.

Mrs Peel   I like keepin' busy.

Beat. **Megan** *stops sowing, sits back.*

Megan   I'm gonna have a baby, Mrs Peel.

Mrs Peel   I know.

Megan   I'm not gonna know how to do things.

Mrs Peel   You'll be fine.

Megan   Most a' things I know you told me.

Mrs Peel   You gonna be good at it, Megan.

Megan *looks at* **Mrs Peel**.

Mrs Peel (*Softly.*) You're gonna be good.

Megan (*Beams.*) You never said that before.

Mrs Peel No. I should a'.

Megan A' we gonna leave together?

Mrs Peel If you want.

Megan We gonna stay together?

Beat.

Mrs Peel If you want.

Megan I do. Where we gonna go?

Beat.

Mrs Peel I spent my childhood in Cumbria. Used to go out on the Lakes with my father on weekends. We'd be out there in all weathers too, hail comin' at us, thunder rollin' in, bitin' winds. We'd stop and eat sandwiches on a brow lookin' out at them moors, at valleys covered in droves a' heather, and fells . . . fells white with snow. If I think about the places I been, and I been my fair share, those white fells a' the loveliest thing I ever seen. I'd like to go there. I'd like to see snow on the fells again.

Megan But there won't be any.

Mrs Peel No. There won't.

Megan But we could still go there.

Mrs Peel nods. *She moves behind* **Megan**.

Megan (*Turns to* **Mrs Peel**.) When a' we gonna leave?

Mrs Peel We' leavin' at sunrise.

Megan Tomorrow?

Mrs Peel (*Smiles.*) Tomorrow.

Megan *turns her beaming face round.*

Mrs Peel *raises the knife and slits* **Megan**'s *throat.*

Mrs Peel *stands motionless for a long time.*

A long shear of light. A series of low concussions.

Mrs Peel *kneels, takes the blade and slits her throat.*

The sun sets. The sun rises.

A shoot grows out of the earth.

Blackout.

peddling

Harry Melling

For the Boy and Margaret

peddling was first performed at the HighTide Festival on 10 April 2014 before transferring Off-Broadway to 59E59, New York, and the Arcola Theatre, London. It featured the following cast and creative team:

Boy   Harry Melling

Director   Steven Atkinson
Designer   Lily Arnold
Lighting designer   Azusa Ono
Sound designer   George Dennis
Dramaturg   Prasanna Puwanarajah

Characters

Boy, *nineteen years of age*
Bossman, *on telephone, voice only*

Note

Each number is a unit of action, not so much a scene.

Play is probably best read out loud.

[1]

The earth grumbles.

Growling. Rising. The city street lamps flicker up.

Loud distorted music blaring out.

In the shadows, between the sparkling orange glows from the surrounding street lamps, we see a lone figure dancing ferociously.

A box-file in his hands.

He's trying to sing louder than the music. Wildly moving.

The music rises into a deep growl.

As we fall into darkness.

[2]

Flicker up.

We're in a field somewhere in London.

Autumn.

Early, early morning.

A half-naked **Boy** *is lying asleep on the grass.*

In his hand a firework.

He sleeps in his own mess. The aftermath of the night before: fag butts, beer cans, a celebration banner, clothes, a rucksack, a stereo, and most importantly an orange plastic crate. In the centre of our stage, amid the detritus, stands a tall wooden telegraph pole.

Long silence.

Boy *sharply wakes.*

Runs to the edge of the stage and vomits once, twice, three times.

Falls to his arse, wipes his mouth.

Silence.

Boy   i –
                 made
                 my –
                 peace
                 with
                 the –
                 worms
                 and
                 the –
                 earth . . .
                 –
                 and
                 then . . .
                 darkness.

Slight beat.

                 'everything gotta start somewhere . . . '
                 they say . . .
                 'everything gotta start somewhere . . . '

Slight beat.

                 as i –
                 waking
                 up amongst it.
                 –
                 up against it.
                 –
                 and on –
                 pinching
                 skin . . .
                 –
                 to try –
                 and make sure
                 i ain't –
                 found my way
                 into an early grave.
                 –
                 but this here ain't a grave.

(nah) –
and this field ain't my tomb.
and even if –
darkness swallows everything . . .
well you can spit me back out again . . .
and see what i do?
–

the grass –
ain't the only thing that's growing –
possibly rotting?
what's the difference?
huh?
–

show me the point in turning . . .
where one thing becomes the another –
something other.

Flicker.

eugh! –
as yet –
another hangover
head-butting glass –
trying to shatter its way out of this –
even he wants more than this –
he getting a bit sick and bored of this.

Flicker.

so i tell them street lamps!
to PIPE DOWN this epileptic fitting!
–

as –
reaching
below me –
i start stirring
the cement of –
concrete London
(which, when) –
swirling, turns this city . . .
it making morning turn into night . . .

and night turn into morning . . .
(like me, you see) –
it waiting . . .
for the daytime to start dawning.
but the world is yawning.
–

it hasn't happen yet . . .
(nah) not just yet.
–

it better happen soon –
otherwise the cement might set.
and then you're really
playing stuck in the mud.
which foot went first?
–

which came first?

He begins to get dressed.

you see . . .
all that's left here,
are my leftovers.
–

and all that's right . . .
ain't necessarily,
the right thing to do.
–

leaving me no other choice –
but to put armbands on (man) –
and jump in!
(even though –
i never learnt to swim)
but fuck it!
it can't be that hard, can it?
it's just a bit of kicking and flapping,
you'll be ok –
as you splashing –
about in the unknown grey –
you trying to pluck hold –

>   of the oncoming day.
>   but you can't reach it.
>   not yet . . .
>   (nah) not just yet . . .

He grabs the firework, puts it inside his rucksack.

>   a long list of yesterdays . . .
>   as the cement begins to set.

Now fully dressed.

[3]

Boy *bashes the stereo's radio on.*

Boy   three yesterdays ago . . .
                  –

                  and there's
                  shitty music
                  on the radio.
                  –

                  as we –
                  holding on to
                  our seats
                  for dear life.
                  in the back
                  of this van.
                  rattling –
                  and shaking
                  on a road
                  (that seems
                  to me) –
                  never ending.

Bashes stereo off.

>   the bossman
>   drives –
>   the magic

white van
that takes
us places.
it takes us places.
–

he lets us
off the leashes
for the races
then afterwards
taking a cut
of my wages.
which means –
if you don't earn hard:
the wheels on the bus, they might not go –
round and round . . .
round and round . . .
all the way home . . .
(yeah) all the way home . . .
praying that my pockets –
they might jingle jangle
with jackpot lotteries
(on that journey home).
that these eyes of mine,
they might turn into pound signs
(on that journey home).

Beat.

there's . . .
(how many?)
one,
two,
three,
four,
five,
six,
of us –
including me –
we all trapped inside
this pinball machine.

–
now –
i don't particularly
wanna know them.
and they don't particularly
wanna know me –
it's not my business
to know their businesses . . .
but to do it –
and get on with it.

Sat-nav female voice: 'Turn left, turn left, turn left . . . '

we're getting closer
to the mystery destination.
i know this because the sat-nav
getting all over-excited.

*Sat-nav female voice: 'Turn left! Turn left! You have now reached your
destination!'*

eventually she climaxing
(so bossman, he pulls over.)

Van pulls up.

tut!
as the boy next to me –
(on purpose) –
he knocking into me –
it making me drop
my young offender's ID.
he tells me i dropped my 'gay card.'
but 'guess what? i don't find it fucking funny!'
'you're the joke,' he says.
'you ain't gonna make none of us any money.'
but i ain't listening . . .
to their sniggering –
and their whispering –
i gotta job to do.

He picks up the ID card.

and so i –
pick up the card . . .
and i attach it to my coat.
(now you see) this makes me legit . . .
with this on –
customers can't question it.

Van door slides open.

(next thing –
you know)
bossman sliding the
magic white van door open
and we file out . . .

He picks up his orange crate. Attached to the crate is a strap, which he hangs around his neck.

hanging these baskets around our necks.
deep breaths . . .

[4]

Boy *addressing each axis of the stage.*

Boy   north . . .
south . . .
east . . .
west . . .

Slight beat.

never . . .
eat . . .
shredded . . .
wheat . . .
(i'm trying to get my bearings –
on the sweet)
but before i can –
bossman, shouting at me from his van . . .
'you better do me proud today boy, otherwise . . . '

Van exhaust.

> and the gunshot go off . . .
> 'so off you fucking trot!'

Van drives off.

> and i well quick out the blocks . . .

He faces north.

> as i –
> making my way –
> through the north London maze of tall hedges.
> and i'm playing a game of chicken with the four
> by fours that try and take me out.
> (they know i'm not –
> from these parts you see)
> so that's why you gotta tread carefully,
> little pedlar boy . . .
> –
>
> *going house to house,*
> *door to door –*
> *knock knocking –*
> *professional doorstop hopping,*
> *hoping that someone might show an interest.*

He knocks.

> 'good evening, sir. hope you're having a good
> one. i'm from Boris Johnson's young offenders'
> scheme. and i was wondering whether or not
> you'd like to buy something.'

> 'i told you already. i told you last week. i know
> your scheme is a scam.'
> –

> and then *bam!*
> he slams the door on me.
> (but that don't deter me.)
> it's water off a duck's back . . .

Slight beat.

and . . .
so i . . .
peddling –
even harder still . . .
down Highgate Hill –
(without no fucking stabilisers!)
i'm not superstitious or nothing (but this time!)
i'm jumping the cracks in the pavement . . .
and i'm trying not to walk under any ladders –
but tricky really in this land of refurb and
scaffolding.
–

as i –
making my way
around the many roundabouts
of Hampstead Garden Suburb NW11.
i'm at house (what?)
number twenty-seven . . .
and i know there's someone in . . .
'cause i can hear them murmuring . . .
'it's him again, don't open it, he'll soon go away,'
they say, but you'll pay . . .

Unzipping flies.

as i –
unzipping my trousers –
'i'm about to take a slash through your letterbox'
. . .
but then their dog comes barking to save the day –
(yeah alright, alright!)
i'll put it away.
–

you gotta . . .
tread carefully,
little pedlar boy.
–

going house to house,
door to door –

knock knocking –
professional doorstep hopping,
hoping that someone might show an interest.

He knocks.

'good evening, madam.'

'hello, Boris?!' says the elderly woman.

'nah, madam, my name ain't boris, we've already
been through this . . . '

He points to his ID badge.

' . . . i'm from the young offender' scheme. i
explained all this to you last time.'

'you've got a pen, then, where do i sign?!'

'nah, madam, there's nothing to . . . i was
wondering whether or not you'd like to buy
something. here we have the everyday essentials:
dishcloths, j-cloths.'

'how much for it?!'

'well, it depends on what you're after madam?
i could do you some j-cloths for . . . '

'how much for all of it?!'
–
and i –
turn away –
cause she senile,
and i ain't a thief . . .

A phone goes off.

He takes his phone out.

(check –
my phone)
there's two hours to go.
and bossman ringing.

Phone rings off.

and . . .
so i . . .
peddling —
even harder still . . .
but no luck at Muswell Hill,
and there's fuck all in Finchley . . .
and now i got a flock of pigeons they all following
me —
they all flapping at me . . .
they trying to scratch me with their mangled feet.
they trying to land their shit on me.
but little do the fuckers know that the human
race considers that to be a good thing, and by
god, i'm still waiting for that pot of gold! so yeah!
that's right! fire away!
—
as i —
making that way down (*ooooh!*)
Bishops Avenue N2.
i'm trying the few . . .
very few . . .
houses that aren't empty.
and how the fuck do these buzzers work?!
all this fingerprint recognition,
it beyond my capabilities.
so i begging the winds,
pretty please . . .
blow their foreign money off the trees!
how dare you pretend to live there!
leaving the rest of us to squeeze into our
cupboard accommodation!
(i said!) tread carefully, little pedlar boy!
this basket getting
heavy around my neck.
behind me —
they're forgotten footprints —

as step, by step, by step . . .
i make my way towards a future!

He turns around.

by –
taking a detour –
down a gravel path . . .
in my hand there's a thousand pebbles –
that i throw into the dark –
and sparks fly!
–

lighting up my feet . . .
urging me forwards,
onwards and upwards . . .
someone soon bound to buy . . .
keep moving –
keep peddling –
all you can do is but try . . .
and hold your head up high . . .
–

going house to house,
door to door –
knock knocking –
professional doorstep hopping,
hoping that someone might show an interest.

[5]

A front door.

Boy *knocks.*

Door opens.

Boy   'hello, little girl, are your parents in?'

               'what's the password?' says the little thing.

Slight beat.

> 'erm . . . is your mum or dad about?'
>
> 'password please?'

Slight beat.

> the −
> little gate-keeper,
> she standing her ground −
> eyeing me up and down −
> (she giving −
> me the once-over)
> and then the okay . . .
> so turning away . . .
> stamping and screaming,
> for mummy. . .

> 'what can i do for you?' says a woman, as she
> descending the staircase.
> −
> (and −
> all the colour
> it draining −
> from my face.)

Slight beat.

> 'are you okay? looks like you've seen a ghost.'

Long beat.

> 'good evening mrs. i'm from Boris Johnson's
> young offenders' scheme, and i was wondering
> whether or not you'd like to buy something. here
> we have the everyday essentials. toilet paper,
> dishcloths, bin bags, bleaches, scrubs, marigolds,
> oven gloves, toothpastes, toothbrushes . . . '

> 'oh no, thank you,' she says, closing the door on
> me.

Slight beat.

He turns to go.

'no wait. wait. here take this.' handing me over a
fiver.

Door shuts.

[6]

Long beat.

Boy   a blast −
from the past.
sending me off piste −
and pissed into the night.
−
now aimlessly walking
trundling and falling −
through leafy London suburbia.
−
with a fiver to my name.
and not even a name to this face.

Slight beat.

i'm just a . . .
professional pain in the arse
selling the means −
with which to wipe your arse.
peddling toothpaste −
to already whitened teeth.
peddling dustpan and brush −
to those who've never had to
clean up after themselves!
−
i mean who the fuck
does she think she is?!
playing the giddy goat with me?
pretending she couldn't see . . .

who quite clearly i am!
—

i shoulda said something . . .
i shoulda given her a piece of my mind.
(it's probably —
not the best of ideas?)
you're not doing so good in here —
you're all the way out where?
—

Hendon?

Sigh.

and —
(yes!) i'm trying . . .
(yes!) i'm trying . . .
to get back on track.
i keep telling myself
i oughta head back.
—

but what's the point —
when you ain't got jack shit.

[7]

North Circular.

Beat.

Boy   and
so i'm . . .
taking a breather . . .
on the north circular.

Slight beat.

and everything gone quiet.

Beat.

Boy *checks his phone.*

(check —

my phone)
there's five minutes to go,
before i need to be at pick-up point.
and six missed calls –
(bossman gonna be pissed.)
so i putting my thumb out to hitch a lift.
–

but no one stopping.
–

all the drivers must be thinking –
my thumbs up –
is a comment on their driving.
but it ain't! –
that couldn't be further from the truth!
in fact i'd rather use a middle finger!
i mean, 'where the fuck is everyone going to?!
huh?!'
and, 'where's my invite?!'

Checks his phone.

(check –
my phone)
and five minutes gone already –
and so now i'm officially late . . .
and for some reason i'm still determined
that some nice driver's gonna take the bait.

Checks his phone.

but another –
five minutes gone past,
and there's no one biting.
so i throwing my arm down,
and i start walking.
–

rattling a toilet plunger
against these rails,
in protest.

Flicker.

[8]

Flicker.

Boy   when . . .
                    between the colours
                    from swooshing cars . . .
                    i see something . . .
                    flashing . . .

Flicker.

                    flashing . . .

Flicker.

                    (is this someone –
                    trying to message me
                    or something?)

Flicker.

                    they should know –
                    that i don't go for any of that morse-code shit.
                    there's no way i'm gonna interpret it.
                    so i carry on walking . . .

Boy *walks off.*

Flicker.

He stops.

                    it being insistent though.
                    with it's flashing –
                    and flashing –
                    and even more flashing . . .

Flicker.

                    'look, what do you want from me? quit flashing
                    your bits at me!'
                    –

                    it getting all suggestive (you see) –

> it luring me –
> calling me –
> taunting me –
> and so like a (something or whatever?) –
> to the flame –
> i follow.

Flicker.

> i follow it all the way to a newsagent's.
> it lives above a newsagent's . . .
> does flick . . .
> flick . . .
> flick . . .

Flicker.

[9]

Newsagents.

Boy   'i'd like to buy a firework please.'

'what's that boss?' says the indian man from behind the counter.

'i said, i'd like to buy a firework please.'

'no, no, boss, sorry i can't do that.'

'what do you mean you can't do that? there's a "fireworks for sale" sign flashing above the shop.'

'no, no, boss, sorry i can't do that, it's after nine o'clock.'

'what do you mean you can't do that?'

'nine o'clock is when my licence stops.'

'well then turn the flicker off.'

'no, no, boss, sorry i can't do that.'

'what can you do?! *huh?!*'

Beat.

> as i –
> walking –
> up and down –
> the fluorescent aisle . . .
> i got me a twelve pack of cans in my hands . . .
> three bottles of wine . . .
> two packets of monster munch . . .
> –

> 'oh and i'll get me three packs of twenty
> cigarettes.'

> 'three,' he says.

> 'yeah. i'm gonna turn every inch of my insides
> black. how much is that?'

> 'forty-two pound fifty-nine.'

Boy *takes off his right shoe and from the inside of the shoe he takes out a wad of cash.*

Offers the cash to the shopkeeper.

> 'go on, take it . . . '

Slight beat.

> ' . . . take it.'

He retracts his hand holding the cash.

> 'you ever heard god click his fingers?'

> 'what's that, boss?'

> 'i said you ever heard god click his fingers?'

> 'i don't get you, boss?'

> 'boom!'

> 'what, boss?'

> 'BOOM!'

Slight beat.

'you see, i reckon that's what it sounds like.
i reckon that i need that. i reckon i need it.'

'what do you need it for, boss?'

'diwali.'

'funny'

'nah i'm deadly serious. i need it for personal
reasons. i think it's about time someone heard
me.'

'heard you what boss?'

'heard me click mine.'

He clicks his fingers.

he makes –
the first move –
leaving the counter . . .
walking over to the shop door.
i think he gonna open it for me –
and tell me to, 'eff off!'
but he don't . . .
he locks it instead.
–

'it's not for another two weeks,' he says. 'but how
can i deny a brother his chance at defeating
darkness.'

'what?'

'deepavali, the festival of light.'

'oh yeah yeah, precisely,' i reply.
–

(it seems –
that luck is –
finally on my side.)

'okay, brother, okay.'
–

as he –

climbing a stool . . .
reaching towards the tallest
cupboard on the wall . . .
–

'here we got the earth-shaker. the onslaught-
maker. the armageddon multi-box. what you
after, brother? a multiple explosion package? or
a single rocket?'

'i want the biggest one you got, brother.'

'it's expensive.'

'yeah, well that's okay. i got paid today.'

He takes out the fiver from his pocket. He adds it to his wad of cash.

he then –
leaving the counter
walking over . . .
with this long elegant rocket in his hands.
–

i mean . . .
it's just –
it's just –
jaw . . .
droppingly . . .
beautiful.

[10]

Boy *takes out the firework rocket from his rucksack.*

Boy   his name's . . .
'atomic meltdown'.
–

and he gonna take down
any who tries to defy me.
–

no one gonna fuck with me . . .
not now.

not with you in my hands . . .
atomic meltdown.
–

you gonna pound out all the fear in me.
we gonna dance cheek to cheek
(i'm gonna . . .
lick your face . . .)
–

me and you we gonna make a noise . . .
so loud!
that no one won't know us!
no one won't know me!
–

atomic meltdown . . .
you gonna sing my name across the skies.
my name will dance in the moon and the stars.
you gonna fill this dark world with bright bright
colour! –
you gonna rip the darkness open!
and everyone that gave me shit will fall into it!
–

atomic meltdown . . .
we gonna start a fucking war . . .

[11]

A front door.

Boy *knocks.*

Door opens.

Boy   'hello, little girl, is your mum in?'

'what's the password?' (*ah!* god not this again!)

'could you get your mum for me please?'

'the password's "open sesame".'

'okay, yeah, that's great, get your mum for me.'

Slight beat.

> the little gate-keeper –
> she standing her ground . . .
> she fully aware there's –
> something funny going down . . .
>
> 'you again?' says a woman, as she descending the staircase.

Slight beat.

> 'yeah, yeah, i forgot to ask you something.'
>
> 'i've already told you, i don't want to buy anything.'
>
> 'i know. yeah, i know. i need to ask you a favour.'

Slight beat.

> 'i need you to swear on your life that you've never seen me before today.'
>
> 'i don't think i have, i'm afraid.'
>
> 'nah, nah, take your time, take your time. this is not a game. i need you to tell me whether or not you know my name.'
> –
> (and she tells –
> the little girl to go upstairs.)

Slight beat.

> 'your name?'

Slight beat.

> 'i don't know your name, i'm afraid.'
>
> 'one last chance.'
>
> 'i think we're done.'

Closing the door.

> 'okay.'

He presents his firework. A flaming lighter in the other hand, the flame dangerously close to the rocket's tail.

'NAH! DON'T SHUT THE DOOR ON ME! IT'S RUDE! this here's a letterbox and it'll soon prove a good shot! you know, i still can't work out if you're taking the piss or not?! i mean how can you not know me?! independent reviewing officer! scribbling your notes down about me. six monthly! bet you that fiver you still got that file-box. oh yeah! filled to the brim it was. filled to the brim! a long list of yesterdays that i'm still swimming in! and don't give me the "we saw so many people bullshit!" because i am not people! i am something made of flesh and blood! peel back this skin, count all the organs i got! someone, somewhere squeezed me out believe it or not!

He sees the young girl through the door's window.

'oh hello, little girl. hello. you gonna open the door for me? the password's "open sesameeeeee!" nah? okay, fair enough, it's getting late. how about a bedtime story to get my point across straight? once upon a time there were three little piggies . . . blah blah blah blah blah blah . . . AND I'LL HUFF AND I'LL PUFF! STAND STILL! CAUSE I'M GONNA BURN YOUR FACE RIGHT OFF!'

Lighter flame about to hit the firework's tail.

Flicker.

He stops.

[12]

Church.

Boy   through –
           the frosted front
           door windows . . .
           –

           i see a reflection.
           –

           not of myself . . .
           and of what i'm about to do –
           (or of what –
           i think i'm gonna do)
           but of myself . . .
           ten or something years old.
           –

           the cute little thing's
           staring at me . . .
           pointing . . .
           tears streaming . . .
           –

           i put my ear to the door –
           to try and hear what he saying,
           but he ain't saying nothing –
           he singing . . .

We hear a young boy singing, 'Lord of the Dance'.

           he belting out a choir tune . . .

Slight beat.

           and i'm in a church.
           –

           the stained-glass window –
           staining my head
           with feelings –
           that i can't pull together,
           (nah) –
           not just yet.

–
as the little me –
he looking right,
then left –
he looking like he lost something,
and so he stops his singing . . .
–

'what have you done with her?' he saying . . .
'what have you done with her?'
–

as he –
taking out –
his very own –
little firework rocket –
he taking aim right back at me –
he rejoining the choir –
he singing it even more defiantly.

Police sirens.

'i'm getting there!' i tell him . . .
'i'm getting there!'
but the police sirens don't care!
as they drown out my explaining.
i tell them to be QUIET!
but they ain't listening
(and why would they?)
they coming for me . . .
–

and so i run . . .

[13]

North London.

Boy   i run –
            i run –
            all the way back
            to where i come from.

(back to what i'm used to –
back to what i'm supposed to do) . . .
–

past the newsagent's
and mistress flick.
who seems to be preoccupied
by yet another prick.
–

and past the pigeons –
who soundly sleeping in their tree.
dreaming that one day –
they might get another chance
to have a go at me.

[14]

Multi-storey car park.

Boy　　　until –
i run (head first) –
into a concrete block.
a multi-storey car park –
that i climb to the top . . . .

Boy *looking for the white van.*

and there's no sign of the van –
i must be what?
two, three hours too late?
–

'oh well, fuck it!'
(it's not my problem is it?)

His phone rings.

He throws down his crate.

Quickly takes out phone.

Hangs up.

Beat.

He then takes a beer from his crate.

Cracks it open. Drinks.

Beat.

Drinks.

His phone rings again.

He answers it.

Beat.

Bossman   boy?

Slight beat.

> i swear to god –
> if you're there you answer this phone.

Slight beat.

> boy?!

Slight beat.

> i can hear you breathing?
> where you hiding?
> you running scared ch?
> balls finally dropped . . .
> and the big bad world too much for yer?

Beat.

> YOU PIECE OF SHIT!
> you piece of shit on my shoe!
> you piece of meat that i eat!
> clap my hands and you're gone!
> click my fingers and you're dead!

Boy *begins dismantling the phone.*

Bossman   i own you!
> i fucking own you!
> and i don't like losing what's mine . . .

        i'm gonna find you!
        i'm gonna find you!
        i'm gon –

Boy *dismantles battery. Phone dies.*

Silence.

He throws the different phone parts away.

Silence.

Boy   so instead –
        i'm watching cars
        reversing into parking spaces.
        (there's something –
        quite comforting in this.)
        so i perform the act myself.

He takes a toilet roll from his crate. He begins to walk backwards marking out a square with toilet paper.

        reversing myself . . .
        (beep . . .
        beep . . .)
        i lie down . . . .
        in a marked bay –
        on the hard grey –
        looking up into
        the dark sky.
        –

        and where the fuck
        have all the stars gone?
        –

        there's not one star left
        or right in the sky.
        maybe they've gone all shy
        and flown away to somewhere nicer?

Drinks.

        somewhere nicer?

Drinks.

> or maybe out of sheer fucking misery
> they exploded themselves
> into dust and rain.
> that one day might hail down,
> and wash away the pain –
> remove the stain –
> of those who only care to gain.
> and yes, yes –
> you're partly to blame.
> –
> you made your bed . . .
> and now you gotta lie in it.

He takes out a cigarette. Lights it. Lies down.

> so stay low –
> and stay stay put.
> stay here –
> and stay safe.
> –
> no one can hurt you.
> (more –
> importantly)
> you can't hurt no one.
> –
> not here.
> not here.
> –
> this is all mine.
> all mine!
> from this line –
> to this line.

Drinks.

Takes a drag.

Blackout.

[15]

Flicker up.

Rain. **Boy** *holds his crate over his head.*

Boy   two yesterdays ago.
                and that shitty weather starts to show.
                it's raining.
                —

                and so i . . .
                thinking about
                running down a level
                to get some cover.
                but i can't leave my parking space,
                (nah) —
                not for another . . .

Drinks.

Blackout.

[16]

Flicker up.

Boy   one yesterday ago.
                and i haven't left my parking space in days.
                —

                which is starting —
                to send me a bit stir crazy.
                —

                i know —
                i should really get back —
                get back to the flat —
                (to pick up my stuff)
                but i can't shift myself . . .
                i ain't got the energy enough.
                —

i got the Gary Guilt –
(you see) . . .
i got it proper bad . . .
Paranoid Pam she coming to stay –
and she won't fuck off –
she won't go away.
–

there was no need to press the button.
there was no need to press it.
–

and now you gone and fucked it.
you can't go nowhere –
cause the bossman gonna be there –
he gonna be running after you –
wanting what's due . . .
his money.
ha!
what money?
i ain't got no money . . .
he gonna have to shake it out of me –
maybe then the penny might finally drop!
and this world of hot air might just pop.
and then all this calamity might just stop.
–

cause at the end of yet another day –
enough is enough!
you're really not that tough . . .
when your pillow is concrete,
and you trying to sleep rough.
–

(that's if –
you could sleep) –
but you can't even sleep.
so i shut my eyes –
and start counting sheep.
–

but all i can see is that little me singing.
was life really that easy at the beginning?

        when all you were worried about was the living –
        not the making of one –
        but just –
        just –
        living (you know?)
        breathing –
        and singing –
        without this tripping –
        sinking, feeling –
        further –
        and further –
        and falling –
        and failing –
        and snoring –
        till . . .

Blackout.

[17]

Flicker up.

Boy *is at the top of the telegraph pole.*

Dreaming.

Boy   i –
        dreamt . . .
        the world
        is just air
        and blue . . .
        –
        no one else.
        just me.
        floating.
        –
        i go to move.
        but i'm quite stuck here.
        up here.

‒
amongst the birds
and the planes ‒
and the clouds ‒
which shifting ‒
revealing . . .
‒
a crowded mass of people
all below me . . .
they all wide-eyed ‒
gazing up at me . . .

Slight beat.

'we present to you . . . THE CONCRETE
BOY!'says a megaphone, and a huge cheer
erupts.

'the concrete who?' i try and say . . .
but my mouth tightly shut.
‒
i try and tilt my head down ‒
but my neck is stiff.
‒
i flick my eyes down a glance . . .
and i'm quite grey and solid.
‒
a concrete god in the sky.
a statue way up high.

Slight beat.

and everyone still down there ‒
standing there . . .
waiting for me to do something.
but i can't do nothing!
‒
i can't even move.

Slight beat.

bossman down there . . .
with all the boys.
–

mrs i.r.o. down there . . .
she scribbling even more
notes about me.
–

the little gate-keeper down there . . .
she doing crowd control –
(and i mean) –
she's much needed.
there's hundreds and thousands . . .
hundreds and thousands all wide-eyed –
gazing up at me.

Slight beat.

'he's not working,' someone mutters . . .
'he's not working,' mutter mutter . . .
'what's the matter?'
–

as –
something –
inside me crunching . . .
it going tick and tick and tick . . .
but there's never a tock!
the crowd are getting restless . . .
'his heart has stopped!'
they shout, they huff and puff and sigh . . .
'what a pointless bloody waste of time!' they all
say . . .
and then they walking away!

Slight beat.

the only person who deciding to stay
is the little gate-keeper.
–

i feel a tug on my laces . . .
and i realise –
that she climbing me.

she carefully . . .
manoeuvring herself over
anti-climb spikes −
which pierce through adidas shoe.
−

when at chest level,
she climbs in.
starts turning −
clunking −
twisting cogs −
winding . . .
−

until −
my concrete heart
starts beating . . .
and my body starts chiming!
and i'm so damn happy . . .
that i could start crying . . .
which i do . . .
−

tears −
turning me −
solid concrete . . .
into cement.
−

cement and rain . . .
that hailing down . . .
washing away
this statue's pain.
−

as the −
little gate-keeper . . .
she jumping out of my chest . . .
she flying through the air . . .
she landing below me in my square.
−

as i −
melting . . .
slipping . . .

further . . .
and further . . .
(i'm not failing!)
i'm just falling . . .
i'm sky-diving . . .
THUMP! –
and the dust goes flying!
until all that's left lying . . .
in the little girl's palm.
–

is a concrete heart.
–

a concrete heart.
now beating.

He is climbing down from the pole.

a concrete heart.
now beating.
–

a concrete heart.
now beating.

Wakes.

[18]

A front door.

Boy *knocks.*

Boy   'hello, little girl? open sesame.'
            –

and the
door opens –
but only slightly.

'go away!' says the little thing. 'i'm gonna give
you to the count of three!'

'nah, there's no need to, little girl. please, will you
forgive me?'

'no! leave us alone! soon mummy'll be home! and then you'll be in real trouble!'

'nah, i don't want any trouble. i just wanna apologise. i wanna apologise for my behaviour.'

'one . . . two . . . ' and the door slams shut.

Loud door crash.

Long beat.

'when i was little boy, little girl, i used to get taken to church by my mum. we would listen to vicar's service. and then at the end we'd all sing a song. i was wondering whether or not i could sing one to you? as a way of expressing how truly sorry i am . . . '

Flicker.

and –
the light –
comes on in
an upstairs room.

Slight beat.

'pooey, you look dirty, you look like you really smell.'

'yeah, well i ain't been home, not in a while now, little girl.'

'well why don't you do that?! maybe you should?!'

'i can't, not yet. first i gotta learn to be good. i need you to help me work. i need to find a different path.'

'you don't need any of that, what you need's a good old bath. were you baptised?'

'erm . . . excuse me?'

'were . . . you . . . ever . . . baptiiiiiiised?'

'erm . . . i don't think so.'

'well maybe you should think about doing that
also. wash away the bad in you. get reborned.
i learnt all about it at school. all you need is a
paddling pool. there's one in the shed.'

'oh, okay.'

'i could do it for you if you like, but not today. we
need to wait for mum to get the garden hose.'

'where's your mum gone?'

'she's gone to waitrose. food shopping. she won't
be long. go on, then, aren't you going to sing me
a song?'

He clears his throat.

*Then presses play on his stereo. A karaoke version of 'Lord of the Dance'
plays.*

'i danced in the morning,
when the world was begun.
and i danced in the moon
and the stars and the sun.
and i came down from heaven,
and i danced on the earth.
at Bethlehem i had my birth.'

dance then wherever you may be!
i am the lord of the dance said he!
and i'll lead you all wherever you may be!
and i'll lead you all in the dance said he!'

*He goes onto all-fours. With his hands he begins to dig up the earth. He
digs and digs and digs . . .*

'i danced in the evening,
when the world turned black.
it's hard to dance,
with the devil on your back.

>they buried my body,
>and they thought i was gone.
>but i am the dance and the dance lives on.'

From the earth he brings out a box-file.

>'dance then wherever you may be!
>i am the lord of the dance said he!'

He lifts the box-file high into the air.

>'and i'll lead you all wherever you may be!
>and i'll lead you all in the dance said he!'

He throws the box-file to the ground. Dust and dirt flies.

Music cuts out.

>and then –
>the little girl –
>she hurls my box-file –
>out her window . . .
>–
>
>'here you go. this is you. mum found it in the
>loft. she read it when you left. she told me your
>father died when you were young, which left your
>mother very upset. she told me the police found
>you in a church singing all alone. and they
>couldn't stop you singing so they took you to
>meet my mum at the care home.'

He is staring at his box-file.

>'i forgive you. you are now forgiven. and as a gift
>i give this to you. be sure to read it carefully.
>maybe then you'll know what to do . . . ?'
>–
>and then –
>the little girl
>she says my name.
>–
>and then i hear –
>my name said once again.

He turns around.

> i –
> turn around –
> and stood behind me
> is mrs i.r.o.
> –
> hands shaking –
> from the weight of her shopping.
> so maybe been stopping
> and listening for a while.
> –
> she hands me a ham and cheese sandwich –
> managing a smile.
> –
> i manage one back.
>
> and then –
> i run –

[19]

Boy *begins dancing around the stage with the box-file, raised up high.*

Boy   i run –
(all the way back
to where i come from –
back to what i'm suppose to –
now knowing what i gotta do) . . .
–
(i'm just)
running and running –
as fast as i can! . . .
you can't catch me! . . .
i'm still a kid! . . .
i ain't a man . . .
nah –
not just yet . . .

(nah) –
not just yet! . . .
the world better get ready . . .
because here i step . . .

[20]

Hampstead Heath.

Boy   into this . . .
             endless green.
             –

             this new found land
             that i've never seen.
             –

             knee deep in long grass . . .
             i striding through this, my heath!
             searching for the perfect patch to plant myself.
             and this . . .
             my teddy bears' picnic.

Prepares his party.

             i'm gonna –
             have a party you see.
             i'm gonna celebrate –
             the last few hours of the old me.

He bashes the stereo on.

Loud music.

Grabs a beer.

Takes out a cigarette.

             and –
             so i begin
             proceedings! –
             by doing what i do best –
             i'm creating a fucking mess!

  –
  dancing and drinking and smoking –
  to loud music blaring out –
  the last few moments of the former me.

A long moment of him wildly dancing.

  (next step) –
  is to climb a tree . . .
  looking over this . . .
  my newly conquered land –
  to see if there's a water supply.
  (and there's many in fact) –
  but one in particular catching my eye.
  –
  then i –
  throwing –
  me down a hill . . .
  unravelling myself . . .
  until i'm at the foot of this pond.

Hampstead Ponds.

He stubs out cigarette.

And begins to undress.

  and stripping naked.
  –
  i put . . .
  my big toe in the water . . .
  it creates a ripple . . .
  which ripples . . .
  and ripples . . .
  it sending shivers up my spine.

Climbs the telegraph pole.

  it's time to put armbands on (man) . . .
  it's time to jump in!

He jumps into the Hampstead Ponds.

  (even though –

i never learnt to swim!) –
but my head's above water –
so i reckon i'm fine!
asking all the ill and devilish things
to leave me behind!
leave me fresh! leave me new!
leave me another pair of shoes
to try and squeeze into!
i beg you to wash away the stench of me!
i beg you to hear me!
i beg you to help me!
scrub me!
scrub me!
scrub me!
clean! . . .
with whatever –
whatever there's to hand –
weeds . . .
grass . . .
stones . . .
until my skin –
red and sore . . .
burnt right through . . .
right through to the core!

He begins violently hitting himself.

scrub me!
scrub me!
wash me!
wash me!
help me!
clean me!
BURN ME!
FREE ME!

He gets out of the water.

and i get out . . .

Long beat.

and . . .
as i begin –
to get dressed . . .
i ain't feeling my best.
–

because i don't feel any cleaner.
i don't feel any better.
–

i just feel completely soaked . . .
in pain . . .
and out of breath . . .
i don't feel born again.
i feel like death.
–

half naked i standing there,
utterly depressed . . .
(until i guess) –
it's time to make –
my way back up the hill . . .
to my so-called perfect patch.
which don't feel so green.
because fuck-all has changed!
i'm exactly the same!
and the only person to blame
it's me and it's you!

He picks up the box-file.

and –
so i (throwing
caution to
the wind!)
–

by doing (even more)
of what i do best!
i'm creating (even more)
of a goddamn mess!

He turns up the volume on his stereo.

Grabs another beer, takes out another cigarette.

Attempts to light it.

>> (even more) dancing
>> (even more) drinking
>> (even more) smoking . . .
> and fuck me . . .
> the world is now turning . . .
>>> my head is now spinning . . .
> –

>> i try and pull . . .
>>> these many swirling
> worlds apart back into me –
>> but they spilling
>>> all over the place . . .

He falls over.

>> i'm in a right sorry state . . .
>>> i think . . .
>> i'm gonna vom!
>>> i ain't feeling so great!
> so you better do it now!
>> before it too late!

He messily opens the box-file.

He rifles through the paperwork. Looking for a particular sheet of paper. Searching, searching, searching, until . . .

He finds the sheet of paper.

Silence.

[21]

*Piece of paper in **Boy**'s hand, raised high.*

Silence.

Composes himself.

Boy   if it was

down to me –
would it be
the birds –
and the bees
or something else?
–

i mean . . .
if i was god almighty himself –
and destroyed
this first attempt at life?
what would my
second version be?
–

a dead end . . .
of endless possibility.

Looks to his sheet.

(you see) . . .
all this time –
unbeknownst to me . . .
been playing a tug of war . . .
with my umbilical cord.
–

it dragging us back to the start.
it taking me home.
–

but how can i even go there?
when all i've ever known . . .
is this . . .
–

so i pull the other way even harder, and resist –
(resist –
and resist) –
it's not so easy –
stepping into the abyss.
–

it's not so easy –
to try and mend and bend –
the smallest moments

in an even smaller history
that might domino me –
into something completely different,
that's not this.
but you are this.
so (again) i pull the other way even harder, and
resist.

He starts putting the other sheets of papers back into the box-file.

(resist –
and resist –
resist –
and resist!) –

He throws the box-file back into the dug-up hole. And begins to re-bury it.

until –
all our cords –
are all twisted and tangled –
we become one big mangled web of people –
all blindly moving –
not realising! –
that when you move one way –
a thousand million others
(including me) we move the other.
we forgetting! –
we all in this together!
one day we might realise –
and change ourselves for the better.

Box-file now buried.

but till that day comes –
i'll make my peace with worms!
and not open this (said) can of worms!
that might eat me?
rot me?
destroy me?
but do please explode me!

He grabs the firework rocket. He then grabs the important sheet of paper. He scrumples up the sheet of paper into a small ball.

explode me! –
into a thousand different pieces of me!

He takes the head off the firework, and pushes the ball inside the rocket.

as all aflame! . . .

Lights lighter.

Plants the firework into the earth, kneels down.

not chasing my tail!

He dances flame dangerously close to the firework's tail.

i fly! –
and at the top of my lungs! . . .
screaming!!!
'EVERYTHING GOTTA START
SOMEWHERE!'
(SCREAMING!!!) –
'EVERYTHING GOTTA START
SOMEWHEEREEE!!!'

He slowly lowers his mouth towards the head of the rocket.

He lights the tail.

The flame rises . . .

Nothing.

No explosion.

Silence.

He collapses. Broken.

The earth grumbles, growling, rising.

The city street lamps flicker.

As we fall into darkness.

[22]

Morning.

A blast of bright sun.

Long silence.

*We find the **Boy** in the exact same position as the beginning of the play. Lying in the grass half-naked with the firework in his hand.*

(As far as is possible) the same mess scattered around the stage as appears in the opening.

He sharply wakes.

Runs to the edge of the stage, goes to vomit, but this time doesn't.

Silence.

Looks to the sun, taking on its bright daylight.

He finds his firework. Dismantles the head of the rocket. Carefully takes out the scrumpled ball of paper. Unfolds the ball, and begins to read.

> 'child and family . . . stand alone form. social services initial report.'

Slight beat.

> 'name of child . . . name (slash) names of biological birth
> parent (slash) parents . . . '

Slight beat.

> 'biological birth parent (slash) parents' home address . . . '

He reads his mother's address.

> 'biological birth parent (slash) parents' home address . . . '

[23]

From his crate **Boy** *takes out a clean outfit.*

He begins to get dressed.

Boy   so i –
              making my way –
              through the south London maze
              of one-way systems.
              –

              and i'm –
              stepping through Lewisham SE13.
              i buy a suit jacket from a charity shop,
              to make sure –
              i brush up clean.

He hangs up his jacket on telegraph pole.

              (and before –
              you even know it)
              i'm gliding through New Cross . . .
              (and i'm –
              thinking to myself) . . .
              i wonder if she gonna look like me?
              laugh like me?
              smile like me?
              i wonder if we're gonna be
              a happy little family?
              drinking tea –
              and playing scrabble?
              we might even quarrel . . .
              but that's alright . . .
              that's all normal.
              –

              and then i –
              walking over Blackheath SE3.
              i'm walking over the burnt-out . . .
              golden grass . . .
              –

            until i finally . . .
            ending up in Eltham SE9.
            –
            i check the piece of paper
            one more time . . .

He puts on his jacket.

Now fully dressed.

            and it's now or never . . .

He hangs his crate around his neck.

[24]

A front door.

Boy *knocks.*

Silence.

Door opens.

Boy   good evening . . .
            miss.

Slight beat.

            and what a beautiful evening it is?
            –
            you may . . .
            or may not . . .
            already know this.
            but i come a long way . . .
            to be here today.
            –
            i travelled –
            through . . .
            cement . . .
            and long grass . . .
            just so's –

i could ask –
you one little thing.

Shaking.

haha! –
and now look at me . . .
i'm all shaking.

Slight beat.

you see . . .
nineteen years ago . . .
i was born . . .
and i didn't grow.
–
nineteen years ago . . .
something happened . . .
and i'm still not . . .
sure . . .
quite . . .
just . . .
what?

Slight beat.

and so . . .
i'm here today.
–
on this . . .
your doorstep . . .
taking this my first step.

Slight beat.

and –
i'm . . .
wondering . . . .
whether or not . . .
whether or not . . .
(i've got a shot at . . .)
whether or not . . .

whether or not . . .
whether or not . . .

He can't.

So instead he presents his crate.

you would like to buy something?

Slight beat.

here we have the everyday essentials.
some might call it . . .
–
life's essentials.

Slight beat.

so what do you reckon, miss?

Slight beat.

miss?

Slight beat.

miss?

Flicker out.

The Big Meal

Dan LeFranc

The Big Meal had its world premiere on February 7, 2011 at American Theater Company, Chicago IL (P. J. Paparelli, Artistic Director). Playwrights Horizons Inc. produced the New York City premiere of *The Big Meal* Off-Broadway in 2012.

The *Big Meal* received its European premiere at the Ustinov Studio, Bath, on 6 March 2014 in a co-production between HighTide and Theatre Royal Bath Productions. The cast and creative team was as follows:

Sam/Robbie/Steven/Marcus/ Jeremy/Patrick/Michael/Sammy Nicole/Jessica/Maddie	James Corrigan
Stephanie/Jackie	Lindsey Campbell
Sam/Robbie	Jo Stone-Fewings
Nicole/Maddie/Jackie	Kirsty Bushell
Pesky Little Girl/Maddie/Jackie	Zoe Dolly Castle and Courtnei Danks
Pesky Little Boy/Robbie/ Sammy/Matthew	Jeremy Becker and Robbie Whittock
Nicole/Alice	Diana Quick
Sam/Robert/Jack	Keith Bartlett
Director	Michael Boyd
Designer	Tom Piper
Lighting Designer	Oliver Fenwick
Sound Designer	Andrea J. Cox

The production transferred to HighTide Festival 2014 on 10 April 2014.

About the Play

The setting is a restaurant in the Midwestern United States, or rather, every restaurant in the Midwestern United States. Some are popular chains, others are more homely; very few are fancy.

There are tables ready to be set. They may be brought together or apart depending on the size of the party at any given moment. Eight actors total. Three men. Three women. A boy and a girl. The server is probably a stagehand.

The actors play the multiple generations of one family as they glide through time (and the guests they pick up along the way). As the characters age, their "essences" pass from younger to older actors. These "passes" ought to be performed as simply as possible. They are designated in the script by the character's name sliding into a new column.

Shifts in time are designated by SHIFT. These shifts can be indicated as subtly or conspicuously as the moment demands, but please try not to overdo the theatrics. These are placed in the script primarily to help the actors, not the audience. We don't want the audience to get lost, of course, but it's okay if they're a little behind the play.

The food probably doesn't look very appetizing. Colorful. Glistening. Grotesque.

Except for a few key moments (and one long stretch towards the end), the play moves very quickly. Pretend the cast is an orchestra tasked to play a piece of music for a conductor whose pace is brisk and unrelenting. Or pretend they're sitting together at a player piano. Or getting their cues from a rapidly scrolling teleprompter. Regardless of which metaphor serves you best, play the action on the line. At performance speed, the play ought to run roughly eighty minutes.

Do your best to cast an ensemble who feels like a family, but don't break your back to make everyone look related.

Let the language carry us through time and space. Don't worry about representing the various restaurants literally. The scenography should probably be a little abstract, allowing our imaginations to leave the confines of a restaurant from time to time. Big scenic gestures should be kept to a minimum (or preferably, completely avoided). As a rule, there should be as few objects flying around the set as possible. The only plates in the play should be the ones that land in the script. The only consumables should be the ones on those plates. Feel free to rearrange the furniture when necessary, but let our imaginations do the heavy lifting.

Lines in parentheses (thus) are meant to be spoken to another character more privately than publicly.

A large generational gap between the actors is important to understanding the story. In other words, if possible cast children in the youngest roles, not teenagers.

The duration of the meals can vary depending on the needs of the production. The first and last meals should probably be the longest. The dialogue might begin over some of the later meals in order to break up the rhythm of the device. But see what works best given the circumstances.

There's a lot of cross-talk in this play and some parts of the conversations are more important than others. Make sure to highlight the parts that are most crucial to the story. It might be helpful to identify the "A conversations" and "B conversations" throughout.

Sound and light cues should be kept to an absolute minimum. There's a moment of dancing that might require a song, but that's about it for sound. Lighting may be used more often, but see how little you can get away with and take it from there.

This is key: all of the actors should be on stage for the entire play. When not in a scene, they are probably sitting in an area where they are removed from the action but can also observe it – actively waiting for their moment to jump in.

Characters

Woman 1 (Older Woman)
Nicole (*older woman*)
Alice, *Sam's mother*

Man 1 (Older Man)
Sam (*older man*)
Robert, *Sam's father*
Jack, *Stephanie's father*

Woman 2 (Woman)
Nicole (*woman*)
Maddie, *Sam and Nicole's daughter* (*woman*)
Jackie, *Robbie and Stephanie's daughter* (*woman*)

Man 2 (Man)
Sam (*man*)
Robbie, *Sam and Nicole's son* (*man*)

Woman 3 (Young Woman)
Nicole (*young woman*)
Jessica, *a gentle soul*
Maddie, *Sam and Nicole's daughter* (*young woman*)
Stephanie, *Robbie's wife* (*young woman*)
Jackie, *Robbie and Stephanie's daughter* (*young woman*)

Man 3 (Young Man)
Sam (*young man*)
Robbie, *Sam and Nicole's son* (*young man*)
Maddie's Adolescent Boyfriends (Steven, Marcus, Jeremy, Patrick, Michael)
Sammy, *Maddie's son* (*young man*)

Girl
Pesky Little Girl
Maddie, *Sam and Nicole's daughter* (*girl*)
Jackie, *Robbie and Stephanie's daughter* (*girl*)

Boy
Pesky Little Boy
Robbie, *Sam and Nicole's son* (*boy*)
Sammy, *Maddie's son* (*boy*)
Matthew, *Jackie's son*

W1 M1 W2 M2 Woman 3	Man 3	Girl Boy

	Man 3	
(*She is setting a table. Not interested in him.*)	(*He is sitting at a table by himself with a drink.*)	
Nicole	**Sam**	
(*She cleans his table, ignoring him.*)	Am I in your way?	
Pretty much.	(*He drinks.*)	
	So what's up?	
Um, side work.	Side work, huh?	
Yeah, 'cause I work here.	Okay.	
And I don't want to waste any more of my life than I have to.	(*He drinks.*) Then don't.	
What?	Uh, If you don't want to waste your life, then . . . don't. It's pretty simple.	
Is it?	Yeah.	
	I mean, no, it's really hard, but it's, uh . . . doable, I think.	
Doable. (*Smiles.*)	Yeah.	
	. . . (*Smiles back uncertainly.*)	
	Is there, like, something on my face?	
SHIFT	SHIFT	
Hey. Sorry I'm late.	Hi.	

W 1 M 1 W 2 M 2 Woman 3   **Man 3**   **Girl Boy**

Woman 3	Man 3
	It's okay. You wanna sit down?
Oh yeah. Thanks.	Here, let me get your chair. (*He does.*)
Oh, you don't have to. Okay, wow, chivalry. That's intense.	Okay –
What's your name again?	My? Sam, my name's Sam.
I thought it was something else.	I'm pretty sure it's Sam.
I'm Nicky.	Oh yeah, I know.
My parents named me Nicole, but just look at what your mouth does when you say it. Nicole. It's weird.	I think it's pretty.
Yeah, you would. You totally would.	Okay.
Well, not, uh . . . All right. So not to be up front, but I, uh, I'm not really looking for anything serious right now.	Oh, yeah. Did it seem like I – ?
No. No, no, no.	
I just wanna be clear, 'cause I just got out of this long-term thing with this total, um, clingy narcissistic asshole, and I'm looking for, you know, someone to pass the time with or whatever, but not like "a relationship."	No, I get it, it's cool.
You know what I mean?	Oh, yeah, "relationships," they're so –

W 1	M 1	W 2	M 2	Woman 3	Man 3	Girl	Boy
					Yeah, it's like I look at my parents and they're, I don't know, intense, I guess, and, uh, hopefully you'll never meet them, so –		
				Yeah, I don't anticipate meeting your parents.			
				This is totally casual.	Yeah.		
					Yeah.		
				So that means if this goes anywhere beyond tonight, which I'm not saying it will, we should keep this as, uh, as anonymous as possible, you know? Like, I don't really wanna know about your life and I really, *really* don't want you to know about mine.	Sure.		
					Oh, okay.		
					Cool, that's cool.		
				(*Pause.*)	(*Pause.*)		
				Oh, oh yeah, sorry, yeah. (*Smiles.*)	But can I ask you what you like to drink? 'Cause I really wanna buy you a drink. (*Smiles.*)		
				Yeah, okay, let's have a drink. (*Drinks.*)	Cool. (*Drinks.*)		
					How is it?		
				Good.	Yeah, I really like this one.		
				(*Pause.*)	(*Pause.*)		
				You wanna get out of here?	Should we order – ?		
					What?		
				You wanna mess around?			

W 1 M1 W 2 M 2 Woman 3   **Man 3**   **Girl Boy**

Woman 3	Man 3
Like right now? 'Cause, no offense, but this date is kinda painful.	Uh . . . I am a male.
Then let's go.	Uh. Yeah, yeah.
SHIFT	SHIFT
Sam.	Hey, Nicky.
It's okay	Sorry I'm –
Yeah, well, I was pretty bored, so . . .	I'm glad you called.
Just a drink. You want one?	Did you order?
	Sure.
(*Drinks.*)	(*Drinks.*)
	This is good.
It's kinda weak.	Yeah. You know, my mom claims to have invented the Cadillac Margarita.
Oh yeah?	Yeah.
Is that a margarita you order at a drive-in, or – ?	No, ha ha, that's funny, but, uh, no. It's just like a normal margarita, but with, uh, a splash of Grand Marnier.
Cool. Cool.	Yeah, she's really proud of it for some reason.
So is your mom like an alcoholic inventor?	(*Smiles.*) Uh, well, maybe like casually alcoholic but no, she's just, she works in restaurants.

W 1 M 1 W 2 M 2   **Woman 3**   **Man 3**   **Girl**   **Boy**

You have a sister?

Yeah, so does my sister.

Yeah. Actually the place where I work where you, um, picked me up – she's the manager, and pretty much the only reason I –

Is that what you'd call it? A pickup? Like I just dragged you out of the bar by your hair back to your apartment?

Ha ha, yeah, kinda. Yeah.
Well, except I was the one doing the dragging

(*Smiles.*) Yeah, yeah.

Hey, do you think your roommate woke up?

I hope so. I hate that bitch.

(*Laughs.*) Why?

She's very, you know (*gesture*), very (*gesture*).
Like this one time my sister came over to cook and she was, uh, wow, okay.

What?

I am telling you stuff about my life. I don't know why I am telling you stuff about my life, 'cause this thing, this thing is not –

Oh.
It's okay.
Totally.

SHIFT

SHIFT

Hey, Sam.

Nicky.

(*They kiss*

passionately.)

She's good. She left this morning.

How's your sister?

Yeah, she liked you too.

That was fun, hanging out. She's cool.

W 1 M 1 W 2 M 2 Woman 3	Man 3	Girl	Boy
	You want a – (*drink gesture*)?		
What do you think?			
(*Drinks.*)			
This is good.	(*Drinks.*)		
	I know.		
Your mom's a genius.			
	You think so?		
This drink's awesome.			
	Yeah, she can definitely make a drink.		
You're kind of awesome too.			
	What?		
(*She makes a face.*)			
	(*Laughs.*)		
SHIFT	SHIFT	SHIFT	
		(*The sound of a child crying in the restaurant.*)	
Is that a kid?	Whoa.		
	Sounds like some kind of freakish animal.	Eeeeeee	
Yeah, have you ever heard a gibbon?		eeee	
	What's a gibbon?	ee	
You've never been to the zoo?		eeeeee	
	Yeah, but –	eeee	
Well, they're like monkeys, but they're apes.		ee	
	What's the difference?	eeee.	
Apes don't have tails.		Ee	
	Really?	eeeee.	
Listen to that.		Eeee	
	Wow.	ee	
Do you like kids?		ee	
	They're okay.		

W 1	M 1	W 2	M 2	Woman 3	Man 3	Girl	Boy
						eeeeeeeeeeeee	
						eeee	
						eeeee	
						ee.	
						Eeeee	
						eeee	
						eeee.	
				I hate kids. They're nothing but, like, snot and shit. Seriously, I think their bodies are literally powered by mucus.		SHIFT	
					(*Laughs.*)		
					(*As if by accident.*) I love you.		
				What?	What?		
				SHIFT	SHIFT		
				Yeah, so I don't know what to do.	She still won't move out? Did you call the landlord?		
				No, she's a freak. (*Drinks.*) Yeah, I called the landlord, but the thing is she's on the lease and she hasn't technically done anything, so there's not much I can –	Okay.		
				Wait it –? No. Sam, this is ruining my life, it is ruining my life. I hate her, I –	Do you think you can wait it out?		
				Really? You'd talk to her?	Okay, okay. So do you want me to talk to her?		
				Okay . . . but I think she's kind of obsessed with you, so don't let her touch your hair or anything	Yeah. I mean it's worth a shot, right?		
				Yeah, a little . . .	She's – whoa – seriously?		
				I mean, can you blame her? (*Makes a face.*)	(*Smiles.*)		
				SHIFT	SHIFT		

W 1 M 1 W 2 M 2 Woman 3

Man 3

So what do you think? Nice, right?

Are you sure we can afford this? It's pretty fancy.

Yeah, I got it.
I mean my credit card's got it, but, whatever, it's our anniversary.

No, you can't pay for this. The glasses are like actual glass. (*Jokingly.*) Anniversary? Is that what this is?

Uh huh.

Of what? The first time we, like, coupled?

Um, no. Of our, uh, (*conspiratorial playfulness*) relationship.

(*Conspires back.*) Relationship? We're in a relationship?

(*Keeps it up.*) Yeah.

(*So does she.*) Holy shit.

I know.

How the hell did that happen?

That's classified information.

I have clearance.

Lemme see it.

(*She lowers a shoulder strap.*)

Good enough.

Now tell me.

Well, first we met.

Then what?

Then we liked each other.

Interesting.

Then we . . . coupled.

I liked that part.

Me too.

And then?

We fell in love.

Oh yeah. That was awesome. What happens next?

I can tell you, but I'm gonna need to see some more

W 1	M 1	W 2	M 2	Woman 3	Man 3		Girl	Boy

Woman 3 / **Man 3**

SHIFT

      SHIFT

You want a drink?

      That's cool.

. . .

      . . .

So what's up?

      Nothing.

Nothing's up?

We haven't talked in a week.

So is there something we need to talk about now?

      Yeah?

Like, I don't know. Anything. Everything.

      Like what?

      Uh . . .
      (*Pause.*)

(*Pause.*)

      What?

What the fuck, Sam?

Say it.

      Say what?

(*She starts to cry.*) Oh my God, say it, say it, just say it!

      SHIFT

SHIFT

      You want another? (*Gestures.*)

(*Shrugs.*)

      So then do you wanna get outta here, or – ?

Look, I can't keep doing this.

      Okay.

We're not involved, but then I see you and then we are and it gets confusing.

I don't wanna hear about your dad.

      Yeah, well, my dad says this thing about healing, how it's like –

W 1	M 1	Woman 2	Man 2	Woman 3	Man 3	Girl	Boy
				You don't even like him.	He's a smart guy.		
				Since when?	Yeah I do.		
				You don't have to like your dad.	He's my dad.		
				Right.	I didn't say I had to.		
				Well, you're a waste of my fucking time.	You're drunk.		
				Forget it?	Okay, then . . . forget it.		
				Is that what you want?	Yeah.		
					Sounds like it's what you want.		
				. . .			
				. . . asshole.			
				SHIFT	SHIFT		
		SHIFT	SHIFT				
		Nicole	**Sam**				
			Nicky, wow, what are you doing here?				
		Hey, Sam.					
		Can I sit down?					
			Uh, sure.				
		Sorry if I'm –					
			No, it's okay. You, uh . . . you look great.				
		Thanks. You look pretty much exactly like yourself, which is a good thing. It's totally a good thing					
			Oh –				

Woman 2	Man 2
	Really? 'Cause I mean, it's been a while.
	How are you?
A little while, yeah.	
Good, I'm good. I'm, uh, here with this guy.	Oh yeah, me too. I mean I'm not here with a guy, I'm, uh –
She cool?	Yeah, she's great. She's very, um, peeing. She's peeing. What about your, uh –
	Good. That's, uh, great. I'm really happy for you.
He's very, um, peeing too.	
(Smiles.)	*(Smiles.)*
(Pause.)	*(Pause.)*
You wanna get out of here?	Well, it was great to –
	What?
This guy sucks.	Whoa. Nicky, hey, look, this woman, she's –
Oh.	No, Nicky, she's –
It's okay. I get it.	She sucks, okay? She sucks, but she's nice, so I feel like I should probably not be an asshole, which I believe is the last thing you called me.
Chivalry.	
Yeah, something like that.	But, um, maybe later tonight you and I can, uh –
SHIFT	SHIFT
Hey.	Did you order?
No, I just got here.	

W 1 M 1 Woman 2	Man 2
	You look, um, awesome as always.
Thanks.	
No, there wasn't much time to do anything but, uh –	So, I didn't really have time to ask the other night –
(*Smiles.*)	(*Smiles.*)
	Yeah.
You got better.	
	Really?
Uh huh.	
	Well, I have been practicing.
Oh really?	
	Sure, but not – not like a lot. I mean, I did keep busy, but, uh, forget it. Reset, ha ha . . . um.
So.	
	How's your sister?
She's good.	
	Is she still working in, um, restaurants, or?
Basically. She's more, like, behind the scenes now . . . purchasing.	
	Cool, cool . . . is she, like . . . married?
Uh, no, no way.	
I mean, why would anyone do that to themselves?	Oh.
Like marriage is so – (*Gestures.*)	Yeah, yeah.
You know?	
	I . . . fully agree.
SHIFT	SHIFT
Sam.	Hey.
Sorry I'm –	It's okay.
(*They kiss*	*across the table.*)

Man 2

Woman 2

What? I do?

Oh, hold on, Nic, you've got something in your hair.

Yeah. Huh.

What is it? Gee, where did this come from? (*He removes a small, shiny ring*)

What, uh, what is that? Sam? What the hell is that?

So I know it might seem a little, um, fast. I mean kinda fast but not really fast, 'cause, well, we have known each other for quite a while, and I know we both have, like, issues with the institution or whatever, but I figure some things are worth the risk.

What are you doing? Sam.

Yeah.

Are you really fucking doing this?

You're not?

Oh my God, Sam, seriously?

Uh, should we order you some? Ha ha.

I'm not wearing underwear.

No, this dress isn't – don't you think I should be wearing underwear for this?

Right.

Don't. Don't say things like that.

Would we have to have a "wedding"? 'Cause I really . . . I really hate weddings. They're so – (*Makes a face.*) You know?

Uh, well, does that mean you're gonna say yes?

I don't know. Now there are people watching. I used to work here. This isn't exactly anonymous. Like that waiter over there? I think I maybe made out with that waiter once. Oh God, I can't believe he still works here.

I know. That's why I'm doing this here. It's where we met.

Yeah.

Really? (*He laughs.*)

W 1 M 1 Woman 2

W 3 M 3 Girl Boy

Man 2

Nicky.

At least don't do the knee thing.

What are you talking about? I have to do the knee thing.

Yeah, but then you're gonna be kinda looking up my dress and that doesn't seem like the most, uh – plus I always thought you might, if you did this, which I never expected you to 'cause that's (*Crazy gesture.*) and I'm not. (*Crazy gesture.*) If you did pop the thing, in my mind I thought you'd maybe

Yeah, okay.

What?

just, like, take my hand and . . . pop the thing but not the thing thing. You'd say something like the thing but better than the thing, way more interesting than the thing, 'cause it shouldn't be like a movie thing, it should be like –

Like what?

like something real, um, beautiful? different? I don't know.

So, um, how about this?
(*He takes her hand, maybe cautiously slips the ring on to her finger.*)

How's that?

Oh Jesus Christ, yes! Yes! FUCKING YES!

(*They kiss across the table like maniacs.*)

SHIFT

(*They curl into each other. Sigh.*)

A little.

You think we're being, like, obnoxious?

Like maybe we shouldn't be making out in public like this?

Probably not

Woman 2	**Man 2**
	(*Smiles.*) If I were in this place, I'd hate us. But we're us, so I'm into it.
Definitely. (*Bites his ear.*)	
	So what do you wanna do now?
Mmm, everything.	
	Everything?
Yeah. Well, except for kids.	
	Right.
'Cause who would do that to themselves?	
	Crazy people, our parents.
I mean just think about it. A whole life with just each other. Think about how fucking rad that sounds.	
	Sounds pretty fucking rad.
Yeah, we could like go places together.	
	You mean like Dayton, or – ?
No, dumbass.	
	Hey.
(*She takes his hand.*) Like places that are really places – like, like Barcelona. (*She pronounces it in a fakey-funny-Castilian accent.*)	
	Barcelona. (*So does he. They keep this up.*)
It is.	
	Wow, that is . . . exotic.
	What does one do in Barcelona?
In Barcelona one can do everything.	
	Everything?
Yes, but in Barcelona, it is not so much.	
	That sounds like a lot.
	(*Laughs.*)

Little Girl (*far away*)   **Little Boy** (*far away*)
Eeeeeeee eeee   Eeeeeeee eeee

Woman 2	**Man 2**
	What was that?
Must be someone's kids.	
	It sounds like some kind of animal.

W 1 M 1 Woman 2	Man 2	W 3 M 3 Girl	Boy
I think they're kinda cute.	You hate kids.	eeeeeeee	eeeeeeee
Me? You're the one who hates kids.	When did I say that?	eeeee	eeee
You know. (*Gestures.*)	Okay.	eeeeeeee	eeee
Yeah –	My body is literally shaking.	ee	eeeeeeeeee
	You wanna get out of here?	eeee.	eee
		(*Closer.*) Eeeeeeee	(*Closer.*) Eeeeeeeeee
		eeeee	eee
		eeeeeeee	eeee
		eeeeeeeee	
		eeeeeeeeeee	
		eeeeeeeeeeeeee	
		EEEEEEE	(*Closer.*) Eeeeeeeeee
		EEEEEE!	eee
			EEEEEEEEEE EEEEEE!
SHIFT	SHIFT	SHIFT	SHIFT
Oh my God.	Whoa.	**Girl** *runs on.*	**Boy** *runs on.*
Who is this? Whose child is this?		*She leaps into* **Nicole**'s *lap.*	*He leaps into* **Sam**'s *lap.*
Hello? Did someone lose a child?	Hello?		
	Did someone lose a child? I've got a parentless child here! Hello? Anyone? Anyone?		
Hello? Anyone?			
Has someone lost a little booger monster? I've got a booger monster here.	I've got a Tasmanian devil who likes to get tickled.	**Maddie** Mom.	**Robbie** (*laughs*) Dad, Dad, no, no, Dad.
Look at all those boogers. (*She tickles* **Girl** *some more.*)	(*He tickles* **Boy** *some more.*)	(*Laughs.*) I don't have boogers! (*Laughs.*)	(*Laughs.*)

W 1 M 1 Woman 2	Man 2	W 3 M 3 Girl	Boy
	You guys hungry?	Yeah.	Yessss.
	Yesssss? Yessss?		Yessss.
	What are you – a python?		
Tamarin. Very good, Maddie, and what's a tamarin got that a gibbon doesn't?		I'm a tamarin.	Yessss.
	What's a python sound like?	A tail.	Yessss.
All right, kiddo, you've won the grand prize.		Is the grand prize crayons?	Yeeesssss. Yeeesssss.
You don't like crayons ?		That's what the grand prize was last time.	Yeeesssss.
	Okay, that's enough python, buddy.		
Well, there's a limited selection of grand prizes these days.		Why?	
	Come here. Sit here next to your dad.		
Well, because of Congress.		Why? What'd the contest do?	Can I get a corn dog?
The contest passed a bill.			Why not?
	No.		So?
A bill's like a Band-Aid.		What's a bill?	Why?
	'Cause you had a corn dog last night	Okay.	
He wants a corn dog? No corn dogs.			Hot dogs.
You know what they're made out of?			
No, they're made out of pigs, and not the nice parts of pigs.		Jennifer's mom has a pet pig.	But I don't like anything else.

W 1 M 1 Woman 2	Man 2	W 3 M 3 Girl	Boy
You like tostadas.	I heard you, honey. What do you want to eat?	Dad, Jennifer's mom has a pet pig	They're all right. I'd rather have a corn dog.
Sorry, kiddo, you're getting something else.		Jennifer says her mom likes to go outside and smoke and talk to her pet pig	There's nothing else to get.
I'm sure you'll find something.	Well, that's what happens when you do what Jennifer's mom did when she was young. You end up talking to your pet pig	I want a pet pig. Can I have a pet pig?	If we had a pig I bet we'd have bacon all the time.
	We don't have room for a pet pig. Now come on, honey, what do you want?	Pigs make bacon?	Yeah, they poo it out.
Hey, Sam? Can I ask you something?	Yeah?	No, they don't.	Uh huh, bacon poo.
You think you can maybe take off work on Wednesday?	Wednesday?	Dad – . . . Daddy, do pigs poo bacon?	Say yes.
(*Smiles. Laughs a little.*) Robbie, that is very funny but very gross. Stop taunting your sister and figure out your order.	Uh, maybe . . . hold on, Maddie.		You're no fun.
It's just this wine-tasting thing – a promo for this new restaurant some of my girlfriends were talking about. It sounds fun.	(*Smiles.*) Hey, Mom? Do pigs poo bacon?	Told you.	She didn't say no. It's still possible.
I work on Thursday.	What's on Wednesday?	(*She colors. Makes sounds.*)	
Because a temp's coming in Thursday and I need to make sure	Okay.	Wah.	
	You can't do it Thursday?	Wah.	
	Yeah, I know, and I work Wednesday. Why can't you take off Thursday?		

W 1	M 1	Woman 2	Man 2	W 3	M 3	Girl	Boy
			So you want me to ditch work so you can get buzzed with your friends in the middle of the afternoon?			Wah.	
		It's a wine tasting.				Wah.	
		Maddie, honey, enough with the – (*Gestures.*)					
						Sorry.	
		It's fine. Just don't do it anymore, okay? Not all sounds are fun sounds.					
		How many times are we gonna make her do that, Sam? Seriously. She's my sister, not our babysitter.	Can't your sister watch the kids?				
			Make her?				
		Well, I think she's beginning to feel a little put out.	She loves the kids, and who wouldn't? Who wouldn't love you little rascals? Huh?				
			(*Makes a pig sound back at him.*)				(*Makes a pig sound.*)
							(*Pig sound.*)
						(*Pig sound!*)	(*Pig sound.*)
		Great. I appreciate it.	Okay, okay. I'll take off Wednesday.				
						No, it's not. It's a pig!	That's wrong.
		Thank you.	You know why? Because you deserve it, you really do.				We weren't doing pigs.
						You were so doing pigs! Dad! Dad! Dad! Daddy! Dad!	
		Just don't make me nag. I hate feeling like a nag.	I'm sorry for arguing.				
						Weren't you doing pigs?	
			Yeah, honey, we were doing pigs.				
		I love you too.	I love you.				I'm reading my menu. (*He does.*)
						See?	

W 1 M 1 Woman 2	Man 2	W 3 M 3 Girl	Boy
(They kiss the air,	*but not each other.)*	Fine.	
Mwah!	Mwah!	*(She reads hers, too.)*	
SHIFT	SHIFT	SHIFT	SHIFT
What are you – a tamarin?	You guys hungry?	*(Monkey sounds.)*	
What is it, Robbie?			Mom.
Hey, you know what an enchilada is? It's a Mexican corn dog			What's an enchilada?
Yep!			It is?
(They secretly high-	*five each other.)*		
Robbie!			But I thought Mexicans only ate real dogs.
Well, that's a bunch of crap.	Nicky –		What? They do! Mexicans eat dogs! It's a fact!
What?	Hey, watch your mouth around him, okay?		It's top secret.
No, listen to this.			It is! I swore!
Where'd you hear that?			. . . Grandpa.
Robbie . . .			
you wanna be grounded?			
Of course, of course you did. Son of a bitch.	Nicky.	Grandpa told me something too. You wanna hear?	
What?			

Woman 1	Man 1	Woman 2	Man 2	W 3	M 3	Girl	Boy
		He's polluting their minds, Sam. Your father is polluting their minds with this this (bullshit).	Not now, honey.				What's the big deal?
		Robbie, what your grandfather told you is a lie, a mean, nasty, terrible lie, and you can never, ever say it again. Is that clear?	I'll talk to him.				Okay, I'll have an enchilada.
SHIFT	SHIFT	SHIFT	SHIFT			SHIFT	SHIFT
	Robert Don't listen to her, Robbie, the enchiladas are terrible.						
Alice Robert. Jesus. There are children at the table.	Well, you're gonna want his meal to get through his asshole.		Dad, come on, we're just trying to get through this meal.				*(Laughs.)*
It's true. I had an enchilada here last time we came to visit and I was clogged up for a week an entire friggin' week!	What?	He said apple.	Dad.			What'd he say? What's so funny? Mom, what'd he say?	No, he didn't.
		Yes, he did.					

Woman 1	Man 1	Woman 2	Man 2	W3 M 3 Girl	Boy
Good God. No one wants to hear about your clog.				Why's he laughing about apples?	Apples of the butt.
		If you keep talking like that I'm gonna make you sit in the car.			Nuh uh.
It's so nice to see you again.		Yes, huh.		I'm gonna have a hamburger.	
You know what you need, Nicky? A Cadillac Margarita!		Oh, you too.		Mom.	
	I remember there being somewhere in the area better than this.	Thanks, Alice, but I've got wine.		I'm gonna have a hamburger.	
		Good. Just tell that to the server when she gets here.	Well, we wanted to take you to that place in the city, but with the kids it's not so easy.		
Maybe you can take us there tomorrow? You talk about it so much.	Maybe you could get off?	(We work tomorrow.) What do we say when we order?	We have to work. I told you that.		
	It's not every day we come to visit.	And?	We can't. You guys know this.	Please.	
Okay. Sorry.		Robbie! Maddie, sit up.	Guys, come on.		Butthole.
(She peruses the menu.)	(He peruses the menu.)	They pull th... d...		But my socks itch.	What? Grandpa said it.

Woman 1	Man 1	Woman 2	Man 2	W 3	M 3	Girl	Boy
(Long pause.)	(Long pause.)	(Long pause.)	(Long pause.)			(Long pause.)	(Long pause.)
							Can I go to the game store?
						Yeah! Can I go too?	
							I wanna go by myself.
		I don't know.					
			You're not buying any more games.				
							Come on, it's just right there.
		You just wanna look?					
							I know. I just wanna look.
						Can I go?	
			You can go if you take Maddie.				
							I just wanna see what's new.
						Can I go?	
							I wanna go by myself!
			Well, that's the deal.				
		Do you wanna go or not?					
							That's so lame.
Oh, let him go.							
							Fine. Let's go.
	Hey Robbie.						
	You forgot something.						What?
	Yeah, you dropped something under your chair.						I did?
	Why don't you look?						
							No, I didn't.

Woman 1	Man 1	Woman 2	Man 2	W3	M3	Girl	Boy
							(He looks under his chair. He finds a simply wrapped box.)
		Open it when you get home.					Whoa. What's this?
							Why can't I open it now?
You know Maddie's asking a very good question, Robert. How come there's nothing for your granddaughter?						What is it? Do I have one? How come there's nothing under my chair? Why didn't I forget something, Grandpa?	
	I don't have anything for her just yet. This one's for the boy. Maddie, no offense, darling, but I don't have anything for you.	Great, just great. Look at her.					(He opens the box. It's an old watch.)
Robert.			Dad.				Cool.
			Dad.				(He puts it on his wrist.)
	Maybe.	(Hey, you think maybe your dad could consider Maddie sometimes?)	Dad.				
	I mean yes. Yes I will, Maddie, and it'll heal the world. It'll abolish prejudice. Are you happy?		Hey.			But will you next time?	Wow, it's got a watch inside the watch.
	Oh, lay off.		Don't screw around.				
The sarcasm, always the sarcasm.	Christ.	Maddie, why don't you and Robbie go to the game store, okay?	These are my children.			(Maddie cries. The others take in this sad sight.)	

Woman 1	Man 1	Woman 2	Man 2	Woman 3	M 3 Girl	Boy
See what you did? You see?	Alice –				No one ever has anything for me.	
Robert.	(*Sighs.*) Darling . . . I . . . I'm sorry. I didn't mean anything by it, I just –	Oh, Maddie, honey, come here. That's not true.	Dad, apologize.			
Young lady!					I HOPE YOU DIE!	
Sam, I hate to say it but we didn't drive nine hours for this kind of behavior. You've gotta get that girl under control. Oh, Robert, hold on, you just ate a whole thing of chips!	Let's just figure out what we want to eat so we can order. Can we order? Ah.	(*Laughs.*)	Maddie! Take that back –! Maddie! Come back here! (*He turns to* **Nicole**.) This isn't a joke. I know, Mom, I know. (*Back to* **Nicole**.) What is wrong with you?		(*She becomes embarrassed by what she has said and runs off.*)	Hey, wait for me. (*He runs off with her.*)
		I'm sorry, but – (*Laughs.*) Where . . . where did you people come from? (*Laughs.*)				
SHIFT	SHIFT	SHIFT	SHIFT	SHIFT	SHIFT	SHIFT
(*She continues to peruse the menu.*)	(*He continues to peruse the menu.*)		At a separate table that is the same table. Oh, hey, Jess. With Nicky's sister.	**Jessica** (*enters*) Hey, Sam. Where are the, uh, bambinos?		

Woman 1	Man 1	Woman 2	Man 2	Woman 3	M 3 Girl Boy
				Oh yeah? What's Nicky up to?	
			My parents are in town, so she's taken it upon herself to vanish. (*Drinks.*)		
				(*Smiles.*)	
				Yeah, parents are intense. I mean, I'm sure your parents are great, but, um, you know what I mean. (*Smiles.*) But does she, uh, does she know we're all hanging out?	
			(*Smiles.*)		
			Who?		
				Nicky.	
			Uh, it's a work party. (*Smiles, matter-of-fact.*) I'm allowed to have friends.	Okay.	
SHIFT	SHIFT	SHIFT	SHIFT	SHIFT	
	And so the guy says, "El barrio? Lo siento, senor! I thought you meant el baño!" (*Laughs.*)	That is funny, very funny. Sam? What do you wanna get?	(*Laughs a little.*)		
Huh.			I don't know.		

Woman 1	Man 1	Woman 2	Man 2	W 3 M 3 Girl Boy
		You wanna split something?	Like what?	
You think the mole sauce has trans-fats?	You've got to stop watching television.			
		I kinda want shrimp.	Okay.	
It's not make-believe, Robert. Trans-fats are killers.	Well, then, let 'em kill you already.			
			Dad, come on.	
Don't speak to me like that.	It's a joke!			
	It's in perfectly good taste!			
		(*Drinks.*)		
Sam, what would that counselor man say? Would he say your father's brutishness is in good taste?				
		Uh, how do you know about the counselor, Alice? (How does she know about the counselor?)	Let's not talk about the counselor right now, okay, Mom? (They asked. What am I sup-posed to do, lie to my parents?)	
Did I say something wrong?	What's the matter? You don't like the guy? I thought you liked the guy.			
		(Yes!)		

Woman 1	Man 1	Woman 2	Man 2	W 3	M 3	Girl	Boy
		Not really.	He's great. You don't like the counselor?				
And what are you gonna do? You're gonna run your mouth.	Now I don't want to run my mouth, but you should know –	No, he's fine, he's – forget it. Why are we talking about this?					
	(Oh, pipe down.)						
	you should know that at this point in your marriage it is perfectly normal to be having problems with physical intimacy.						
Robert.			Dad.				
	Now hold on, look, I know you kids love each other very much, but they don't call it the seven-year rash for nothing						
	What?	Oh my God.					
Itch.							
Itch. It's called the seven-year itch.	Of course it is. What did I say?		Twelve years, Dad. We've been married twelve years.				
You said rash.	Well, you know what? It feels a lot more like a rash. I think rash is better.						
SHIFT	SHIFT	SHIFT	SHIFT				

Woman 1	Man 1	Woman 2	Man 2	Maddie (W 3 M 3 Girl)	Robbie (Boy)
				(runs in) Mom, Dad!	*(runs in)* Dad!
				I need to tell you something.	She's lying. Don't listen to her; she's totally lying.
			Guys.	Robbie pushed me.	Seriously, don't listen to her, she's not telling the truth. I would never do something like that! Why would I do that? I love her, she's my sister, I love her more than anything. She's my sister. Why would I do that?
		Hey.		Yes, he did. I was looking at the princess movie and he told me you can see the princess's boobs in this other movie where she does it with a pirate who does it with other pirates and I said, You're lying, the princess wouldn't do that, and he said, No I'm not, and so I said, How would you know? Do you do it with pirates who do it with other pirates? And then he pushed me!	
		Calm down.			
		You need to slow –	What happened?		
	Wohoho.				
		I can't understand.	Did you push her?		No I didn't. Dad, you have to believe me!
		Hey.	Well, it sounds like –		
		We shouldn't have let them go.		He shoved me.	I didn't push you!
Is she scraped? It looks like she's scraped!		She's fine.			See? She's already changing her story. That means she's lying
Are you sure?		Yes, they fight, it's fine.			

Woman 1	Man 1	Woman 2	Man 2	W 3 M 3 Girl	Boy
		Everything's fine.	Cut it out. Listen to me.		You're a compulsive liar and you're too dumb to even know what compulsive means.
			Hey! Both of you, calm down.	I hate you, Robbie, you're the devil and you have boobs.	
					Unlike you.
				Take it back.	You told Grandpa you wanted him to die.
		Guys! Hey! Do you want to be grounded? 'Cause you keep acting like this, that's exactly what's gonna happen.		You just like him 'cause he gives you stuff	
		(She's livid, but tries with all her might not to respond.) *(Pause.)*	*(Pause.)*	*(Pause.)*	*(Pause.)*
Ooooh, watch out, kids. Here comes big momma. *(Laughs.)*					I'm gonna go play video games across the street.
				Where?	At Lamppost Pizza.
(Pause.)	*(Pause.)*			I'm coming	No you're not.

Woman 1	M 1	Woman 2	Man 2	Woman 3	M 3	Girl	Boy
						I have quarters.	Fine.
						(She goes.)	*(He goes.)*
		(Takes a drink.)	*(Squeezes* **Nicole***'s shoulder.)*				
SHIFT			SHIFT	SHIFT	SHIFT	SHIFT	SHIFT
				(Laughs.)			
			— and so the guy says, "El baño? Lo siento, señor, I thought you said . . . EL BARRIO."				
			(Laughs.)	*(Laughs.)*			
			Or, uh, maybe it's the other way around. I don't know.				
				That's good.			
			Yeah.				
				Barrio, that's funny.			
			Thanks, yeah . . . Nicky thinks it's racist.				
				Well, it is a little racist.			
			Sure, a little. Yeah, I guess.				
				But that's what makes it funny. I mean, it's racist, but it's not offensive or anything.			
			"EL BARRIO!"				
				Ha ha.			
			No harm, no foul, right?	Right.			
			(Smiles.)	*(Smiles.)*			
				Lemme see your hand.			
			Why?				
				I wanna read your future.			
			You're into that crap?				

Woman 1	Man 1	Woman 2	Man 2	Woman 3	M 3	Girl	Boy
				Come on, hand it over. (*She grabs his hands. Studies them.*)			
			Seriously?				
			What does it say?				
				Hold on.			
				I don't know.			
			Well?				
			What do you mean you don't know?				
				I'm new at this, okay? (*Laughs.*)			
			Talk about a tease. (*Laughs.*) (*He lets go of her hand.*)				
				Hey, so I was gonna go to this show.			
			Oh yeah?				
				Yeah. These friends of mine, they're supposed to be good.			
			Cool. Sounds like your friends are pretty cool.				
				Oh yeah, big time . . . you wanna tag along?			
			Tag along? Like go with you?	Yeah.			
			Oh, uh – (*Smiles.*)				
				You don't have to. (*Smiles.*)			
			I know I don't have to I mean I want to, but, uh –				
		(*Drinks. She might absentmindedly pick some lint off his shirt. Something domestic, common, none too intimate.*)	(*Smiles.*) uh –				
			I'm, um . . . I'm . . . married.				
				Yeah, I know.			
(*Continues to berate.*)	(*Continues to berate.*)		I'll	What's that have to do with – ? Wait, what did you think I was asking ?			

Woman 1	Man 1	Woman 2	Man 2	Woman 3
			(*Smiles, embarrassed.*) I didn't think you were – no, look, Jess.	
				It's a concert, Sam.
			I know	
				I'm not some slut.
			Whoa, hey, I didn't say you were.	
			Sure.	You're the one who started hanging out with me, so don't start acting like I'm the one doing something inappropriate here.
			Hey, can we chill out? No one's doing anything.	What did you think was happening?
			(*Smiles.*) I, I didn't think anything was happening.	
			Yeah.	Oh?
			(*Nervous, excited by her interest.*) No, what – was I supposed to think that?	(*A grin.*) Nothing was happening? Nothing?
SHIFT	SHIFT	SHIFT	SHIFT	SHIFT (*Exits.*)
Well, I'm not!	We're ready to order!		Hold on a sec, Dad.	
	Come on, we haven't got all night.	I just need another minute.		

Woman 1	Man 1	Woman 2	Man 2	W 3	Girl	Boy
	Well, then, I'm gonna order. I'm about to eat your mother's head.		Fine, if you feel like you can't wait.			
Hey!						
	That's exactly what I feel like.					
SHIFT	SHIFT	SHIFT	SHIFT		SHIFT	SHIFT
(At the same table but not in the same scene as M2 and W2.)	*(At the same table but not in the same scene as M2 and W2.)*				*(She runs in. She sits at the table. Colors. Same table but not the same scene.)*	*(He runs in. He sits at the table. Colors. Same table but not the same scene.)*
		The two of us?	So . . . uh . . . I was thinking maybe we could find some time to get away, just the two of us.			
		You hate vacations.	I love vacations.			
		All you did in Barcelona was watch TV.	Ohhh.			
		Why?	What?			
		Why? Why a vacation? Why now?	I don't know, I thought it'd be fun. I thought it'd be – We could have some time for just you and me, the two of us, and – what?			
		Uh huh.				
		I saw you.				
		Don't give me what.				
		At that restaurant with that, that girl—	What are you talking about?			

Woman 2	Man 2
	What girl?
Oh, fuck you. What girl – fuck you.	I don't know what you think you saw, but –
With the jacket, the cute little – and the hands. I saw her holding your hand. I saw her whispering.	Okay, hold on.
	Nicole.
She's the one from work, right?	Listen, please listen.
You had your hand on her thigh.	Nicole.
You are –	Hey,
	I can explain, I can –
you are such an asshole.	Hey, we're, we're in public.
Fuck you, fuck you.	It was nothing, honey, it was, hey, we didn't even –
I don't care.	I, I did not act on the –
Let the world know what a fuckin' asshole you are.	not that there was anything to act on –
What? What were you so brave not to act on?	Okay, there were feelings. There were feelings, but feelings alone are not –
I'm taking the kids and we're going to my sister's.	Hey, hey, no. My parents are coming in to town next week. This is not the time to –
Oh, so I can just grin and bear it through another fuckin' meal with that condescending fuckin' asshole and his miserable wife.	No, so the kids can see their grandparents, so they –
Oh, the kids don't like your parents either.	That's not true.
They're pests.	That doesn't matter. What matters is –
Your mother, last year she sat them down and made them write birthday cards to your father 'cause they forgot.	Well, that's good; they should remember his birthday, he's their grandfather.

W 1   Man 1

Woman 2

Man 2

Woman 2

They're children.

Man 2

That doesn't mean they don't have an obligation –

Woman 2

You don't like him either.

Man 2

Yes, I have issues with my father, but those issues don't mean that my children –

Woman 2

Look, you've met someone. I . . . I've sort of met someone.

Man 2

You don't –
What? You what? Who? Who did you "meet"? Nicky? What is going on?

Woman 2

So let's just walk away and start over. Let's – (*Near tears, guilt-ridden.*) I'm sorry, Sam.

Man 2

You can't do this.
No.
No.
Nicole, look at me.

Woman 2

My sister's agreed to let us live with her until I can find a job

Woman 2

I've made up my mind, Sam.

Man 2

Come on, hey, look at me.

Woman 2

No. No. I won't.

Man 2

Listen, just listen.

Woman 2

I, I'm miserable, Sam, miserable! No, I will not –

Man 2

Nicole,
Nicky,
please.

CLANG.

(*Unbeknownst to everyone else,* **M1** (*as* **Robert**) *is served a big plate of food. It's heavy. It makes a big clang sound when it hits the table. The clang shakes the table.*

Woman 1	Man 1	Woman 2	Man 2	W 3 M 3 Girl	Boy
	He begins to eat his food. Everyone else at the table notices him eating. They stop what they're doing. They avert their eyes. No one looks at **M1**. *He doesn't care. He keeps eating. He takes his time. He leaves the table when he's finished.*				
SHIFT	SHIFT	SHIFT	SHIFT	SHIFT	SHIFT
(*Long, long pause.*)	(*Long, long pause.*)	(*Long, long pause.*)	(*Long, long pause.*)	(*Long, long pause.*)	(*Long, long pause.*)
(*Very, very shaken.*) Robert . . . Oh, my dear, dear, dear . . .		I'm sorry, Sam. I'm so sorry.	(*He is very very shaken . . .*)	What's wrong?	What's the matter?
		(*She takes Sam's hand.*) I'm not going anywhere, okay? I am right here. Maddie, not now.		Dad? I'm sorry. I didn't really want Grandpa to die. Dad? I take it back. I really liked Grandpa.	
		Why don't you kids color, okay? (*She keeps her hand on* **Sam**'s.)	(*He is staring off, not really noticing* **Nicole**'s hand.)	Grandma? You know I didn't mean to, right? I didn't mean to, I didn't mean to, I didn't – (**Maddie** *runs off.*)	Hey, wait for me. (**Robbie** *runs off.*)
SHIFT	SHIFT	SHIFT	SHIFT	SHIFT	SHIFT

W 1	M 1	Woman 2	Man 2	Woman 3	Man 3	Girl	Boy
				Maddie (*runs in*) Mom, Dad, is this true? Are you seriously letting this happen?	**Robbie** (*runs in*) Hey, wait. Dad, she is freaking out – I just brought up the car thing casually and she went off on me.		
Hey, calm down.							
			Is what true?	With the car?			
Guys, we're in public.			Yeah, what's the problem?				
				Oh my God, why does Robbie get the Nissan tonight?	I have a student-council meeting.		
Maddie.			He's got a student-council meeting.				
				And you buy that?	What is this, Nuremberg?		
Honey –				Like you know what that is.			
			Robbie, do you or don't you have a student-council meeting tonight?	Come on, I have a thing tonight. Jennifer's mom let her have the car and he's lying.			
					Yeah, I do. Of course I do. I'm in student council, we have meetings. Why wouldn't I have a student-council meeting?		
				On a Friday night?	It's a social meeting.		
Guys, come on, give it a rest.			See?	Oh, okay, a "social meeting" –	There's a swimming pool, there are parents.		
				More like suppliers.			
Watch your –			Hey! Robbie! That's your sister!				

W 1	M 1	Woman 2	Man 2	Woman 3	Man 3	Girl	Boy
				See? He's an asshole. I don't get why he gets to have the Nissan whenever he wants.			
		It's not whenever he wants.			I have meetings for my future.		
				Last time you had a meeting for your future you crashed the car.			
		(He crashed the Nissan?)	(A scratch – he scratched it.)		I didn't crash the car.		
		(I didn't know that.)	(It's not a big—)	Then what do you call it when your car runs into a fence? Is that like how people park in the future?			
					I barely hit the fence.		
		Robbie, you hit something with the Nissan?		You smashed the passenger-side door.	No, Mom, I just dented it a little.		
				Yeah, sure. My friends can't get in that way now. They have to climb over me.			
					More like climb on top of you.		
				What?	(Gives his sister a knowing look.)		
		(Oh God, I don't even wanna know.)	Maddie, cut it out.	Oh, okay. Hey, you guys wanna hear why Robbie crashed the car?			
				Why?			
		Your brother is taking the car tonight. You get it tomorrow night. That's that.		But I'm not doing anything fun tomorrow night. I'm doing something fun tonight. Jennifer's mom let her go and			

W 1 M 1 Woman 2	Man 2	Woman 3	Man 3	Girl Boy
		Robbie's lying. Look at him – he's a liar.	(*Victorious.*) Thanks, guys, gotta go. (*Gathers his stuff.*)	
	This isn't about Robbie.	That's a first.		
	Is the attitude really necessary? There's one car and two of you. What are we supposed to do?		I'm gonna be late. Later, Maddie. (*He exits.*)	
Be careful!		Yeah, great. Don't die, 'kay? Cool, I like you so much.		
(*Pause.*)	(*Pause.*)	(*Pause.*)		
	(*He turns to* **Nicole**.)	(*She seethes, having been left with her parents in a cheesy restaurant far away from her friends.*)		
	Hey, did they raise the price on this sampler platter?	(*Rolls her eyes. Jiggles her leg. Growls.*)		
Huh, that's a drag				
SHIFT	SHIFT	SHIFT	SHIFT	
		Okay, guys.	**Steven** (*enters*)	
Oh! Hey, Steven. Maddie's told us so much about you.		(*Sighs. Smiles. Hopeful.*) So this is, um, this is Steven.		
	I'm Maddie's father. Sam.	It's Madeleine, Mom, not Maddie . . . Jesus.	It's really good to meet you, Mrs. –	
Call me Nicole. (*Smiles.*				

W 1	M 1	Woman 2	Man 2	Woman 3	Man 3	Girl	Boy
					It's so nice of you guys to take me out to dinner.		
			What? I thought you were paying.				
			(*Laughs.*) Ah, I'm just pulling your leg, Steve.				
			Sorry. I guess everyone's just growing up too fast for me.	His name's Steven.	It's okay.		
		(He's cute.)		(Mom.)			
			So what are your interests, Steven?	Steven's really talented –	Well, I'm really into music –		
			A musician.		Kind of –		
			Oh yeah? What do you play?		Guitar, mostly, but I can also play drums a little.		
			Cool, very cool. Well, it looks like you have yourself a pretty cool guy, Maddie.	Thanks.	Thanks.		
		How did you guys meet?		At a party at school for Spanish. We're in Spanish together. For Cinco de Mayo.	At a party.		
			Well, I met Maddie's mother while she was waitressing.		Oh.		
		Sam.	It's true! We weren't much older than you two. You kids should've		Cool.		

W 1	M 1	Woman 2	Man 2	Woman 3	Man 3	Girl	Boy
			seen her. She was gorgeous, and I went right up to her. And lemme tell you, Maddie, your mother wasn't exactly looking to settle down. I mean, the first date alone was (*Laughs.*) well –	Okay, we don't need to hear about how you, like, conquered Mom.			
		That's not really how it happened at all. Maddie, don't listen to this. Sam, please.					
			All right, all right.				
			So, Cinco de Mayo, huh? Are you, uh . . . Latino, Steven?		Um.		
					I'm adopted, so I don't really know, but I sort of doubt it.		
			You know, my dad used to tell this joke about Latinos . . . it's not offensive, but it's a little racy –				
				Dad.			
			Okay, okay. (*Makes a whip sound as if he's fighting off lions. Laughs.*)				
			Well, despite what these ladies might tell you, my dad was quite the comedian.				
					Wow, I, uh, I can't wait to meet him.		
			That's nice of you to say. But my dad passed away a long time ago.				
		Sam.					
					Oh, I'm sorry.		
			It was a long time ago.				
					Still, that really, um, sucks.		

W 1	M 1	Woman 2	Man 2	Woman 3	Man 3	Girl	Boy
			(*Smiles.*) Yeah, well, we'll all get there someday.				
				Dad.			
			What?				
				You're being morbid.			
			Who's being morbid? Death's a part of life, am I right, Steve?				
		SHIFT	SHIFT		SHIFT		
			Then who's Steven?	His name's Marcus, Dad.			
		Where are your parents from, Marcus?			**Marcus** Ohio.		
				That was – what is wrong with you?!			
			Buckeyes.		Okay.		
		SHIFT	SHIFT	SHIFT	SHIFT		
				Jeremy doesn't like football.			
			Who doesn't like football?				
				He plays tennis.			
			Oh yeah?				
				Jeremy's really talented, Dad.			
			What position?				
					Jeremy Um, there's kinda like only one position.		
			Mm, well, what should we have to eat? Anyone want an appetizer?				
				(Mom.)			
		Don't listen to him. (He's cute.)					
			You want calamari?				
					Oh, I'm allergic. Sorry.		
			To calamari?				
					To shellfish.		

W 1	M 1	Woman 2	Man 2	Woman 3	Man 3	Girl	Boy
			Then why can't you eat calamari?				
		(*Laughs.*)	Is calamari a shellfish?	Yes.			
		Oh, Sam.	Excuse me, excuse me! Am I talking to you? No. I'm talking to, uh, uh, Patrick, right?	Patrick. Oh my God.			
		Hey, don't talk to me like that! How dare you?					
		SHIFT	SHIFT	SHIFT	SHIFT		
		Don't talk to me that way.	Now, Patrick, I thought calamari was a-a-a octopus.	It's squid.	**Patrick** It is, but –		
		Sam.	Okay, squid, but I don't see what a squid has to do with a clam or an oyster or what?				
		Sam. Apologize.	For what?	Stop, please stop. We're in public. Oh my God, can't you guys be normal for just like one meal? I knew this would happen. This always happens.			
		First of all, for your tone.	Tone. What tone?				
		The way you spoke to me and Maddie was totally disrespectful.		This was a bad idea. I'm sorry, I'm really sorry they're being like this. But it's not okay. They're always like this.	It's okay.		
		We were not mocking you.	You were mocking me – both of you were mocking me and I'm supposed to respond in a respectful way when I'm shown little to no respect myself?		It's seriously okay.		
		Sam.					
		We weren't the ones being disrespectful.					

W 1	M 1	Woman 2	Man 2	Woman 3	Man 3	Girl	Boy
			Then what do you call that "Oh, Sam," with the little laugh?	Maybe we should go.	We don't have to do that.		
			If that's not mocking, then I don't know what is. Wait, wait, did she —	I'm telling you I want to go.	Okay.		
		Go? What do you mean, go?		We're going. Yeah, we're gonna go.	It was really nice meeting you guys.		
			You can't go.	I mean me and Patrick are getting the hell away from this whole dysfunctional situation.	I think since we're going, I should really pay you guys for my meal.		
		Dysfunctional?		Yeah. Dysfunctional.	**Michael** My name's Michael.		
		You think this is dysfunctional? God, you're spoiled, you know that?	No, no. Patrick		SHIFT		
		SHIFT	SHIFT	SHIFT			
		You don't know a thing about dysfunction. Just take a look at the world. Look at all the terrible things happening in the world and tell me that this, this is dysfunctional. If anything, you should feel blessed.	Right, right, right. Michael, you're not gonna pay, okay? This is on us.	Oh yeah, this is good. You're not dysfunctional 'cause there's like apartheid or something happening in some impoverished nation.	No, please, just lemme give you guys a little.		
			No, no. Thank you, but no.		It's okay. My parents gave me some money.		
			Well, that is certainly generous of them, but we've got it covered.	Blessed? Wow. Blessed. Okay.			

W1 M1 Woman 2	Man 2	Woman 3	Man 3	Girl Boy
Yeah, get sarcastic. That helps.	It's very nice to meet you, and I want to apologize for the way my daughter is behaving, but –	Me? Why are you apologizing for me? You're the one acting like a freak.	Um. Okay . . .	
	A freak.			
Sam, she's right, you were not –	Okay.			
What?	Why don't you just order another drink?			
	My mother's right. You're more fun when you're drunk.			
(Horrible pause.)	(Horrible pause.)	(Horrible pause.)	(Horrible pause.)	
(She is rattled . . .)	(. . . He is embarrassed . . .) Hey, ah, Nicky, I'm sorry. I didn't –			
Don't.	After what I did? What did I do?	Seriously, Mom, I can't believe you let him talk to you like this after what he did to you.		
Maddie.	(Pause.)	(Horrible pause.)		
(Pause.)	Nicole?			
	What did I do?			
Sam.	You wanna fill me in here?	I'm sorry, Mom. I didn't mean to – Mom – I didn't mean to – (She goes.)	(Pause.)	
Sam.	Huh?		(He goes.)	

W 1	M 1	Woman 2	Man 2	Woman 3	Man 3	Girl	Boy
			You wanna fill me in here on what I did? (*He slams the table with his palm.*)				
		SHIFT	SHIFT	SHIFT	SHIFT		
				Stephanie (*enters, bright and cheery*) Oh my God, hiii!	**Robbie** (*enters*) Hey, Mom, Dad. Um, well, this is Stephanie. *hands.*)		
		Hey, Robbie.					
			stands up	*to shake*			
		(*And everyone* Oh, hey, Stephanie! I'm Nicole. We've heard so much about you.		It's so nice to meet you guys.			
			Stephanie? What happened to Marissa? (*Laughs.*)		Dad.		
			I'm just pulling your leg, Steph. Marissa doesn't exist – well, at least not to my knowledge. Maybe Robbie's got a secret Marissa under the table. Watch out for this one. (*Laughs.*)		Robert. My name's –		
			Oh, I'm just having some fun.		Dad.		
			Call me Sam.	Thanks, Mr. – Thank you so much. Sam.	It's not funny.		

Woman 1	M 1	Woman 2	Man 2	Woman 3	Man 3	Girl	Boy
			(Hey, way to go, Robster) (*Sizzle sound.*)		(Dad.)		
SHIFT		SHIFT	SHIFT	SHIFT	SHIFT		
Alice (*enters*)							
I want a picture! Hello? Picture time!			Mom.		Grandma.		
Oh, shut up. I want Robbie and his new girlfriend for my wallet. Saaaay nacho!				Nacho.	Nacho.		
SHIFT		SHIFT	SHIFT	SHIFT	SHIFT		
		Oh, I like her, Robbie. I like her a lot.			Yeah, me too.		
You know, girls these days lack poise, they lack class. But Stephanie, that is a very classy young lady.		I don't usually like "girly" girls, but that Steph, she is something else. (*Laughs.*)			Okay.		
Absolutely adorable.		Just don't fuck it up, okay? Men tend to fuck things up for themselves, especially when they're happy.			Cool.		
					Thank you.		

Woman 1	M 1	Woman 2	Man 2	W 3	Man 3	Girl	Boy
Your mother's right.					Right.		
		God, I hope you're using condoms. You're using condoms, right? Sorry, I'm sorry, but I have to ask.			Yeah.		
					Mom.		
					Or not.		
SHIFT		SHIFT	SHIFT		SHIFT		
					(**Robbie** *adjusts his wristwatch nervously.*)		
			So what's up?		Um, so what do you think of her, Dad? I mean, really.		
			Stephanie? She's great. She's a very nice girl.		And?		
			And, well, she's young.		She's just two years younger than me.		
			You're young too, Robbie.		You think everyone who's not old is young. I'm very professional for my age.		
			All I'm saying is now is maybe not the time to be settling down.		Well, when's the time? When you say so? I've got plans, Dad. I've got ambitions. Play the field? Uh, wow.		
			No. I just think you should play the field a little. I mean, let's be honest, Robbie, you met this girl in high school.				

Woman 1	M 1 Woman 2	Man 2	Woman 3	Man 3	Girl	Boy
				And you met Mom at a bar. What's wrong with high school?		
		Restaurant. We met at a –				
		Nothing, there's nothing wrong with it, it's just –		I love her.		
		You – ?				
		Okay, sure, you love her and that's, that's real to you right now at this age, but –		Yeah. It is. No, at any age. It's real. This is what I want.		
		Sure, of course, sure, but –				
			SHIFT			
			(*She clinks a glass.*)			
		Robbie.	Excuse me!			
		SHIFT	Hi!			
			Excuse me! Um, hi.			
			So Robbie and I have a little announcement.	SHIFT		
		An announcement?				
			Um, you wanna?			
			Okayokayokay . . . WE'RE ENGAGED!	Yeah. Go ahead.		
How wonderful! How absolutely wonderful!	Oh, honey! That's great! That's so great!	Wow, that is very . . . wow.	Thanks. Thank you.			
			(*She runs over to the ladies.*)			

Woman 1	M 1	Woman 2	Man 2	Woman 3	Man 3	Girl	Boy
A wedding! I love weddings!		(*Hugs her.*) Welcome. Welcome to the family!	(*And the*	*drinks start*	*flowing*)		
				Thanks. Um, Mom? Is that okay? Can I call you Mom?			
		Mom? Wow! I guess I kinda am – Yeah, go for it!	Hey, I, uh, thought we were gonna talk about this some more, buddy.				
					Why? I've made up my mind.		
			Of course you have. I just want you to know that I'm always here to help you make your own decisions.				
					Dad, I'm getting married.		
		Oh, I love this girl. Don't you love this girl, Sam?					
					She's the love of my life.		
			I know, I know. She's very nice.				
		When's the wedding?	And why wouldn't she be?				
				We don't know yet, but we're thinking maybe Valentine's Day.			
Valentine's Day!			That is definitely a romantic day.	Kissed.	Yeah it's the first day we, uh – kissed.		
		Wow!					
Do you have a dress?		Oh, God, you should've seen mine. I don't know what I was thinking		Not yet.			

Woman 1	Man 1	Woman 2	Man 2	Woman 3	Man 3	Girl Boy
When you order the cake, don't forget that I'm allergic to walnuts and marzipan.					(Dad, can you please say something?)	
			(Of course, yeah.) (**Sam** *stands, toasts.*) Uh, Stephanie, honey, hey, congratulations.			
				(*She practically tackles* **Sam** *with a hug.*) Oh my God, thank you, thank you so much. (*She is suddenly crying*) Yeah, it's just I'm so happy.		
			Are, are you okay?			
		Sam.	And your dad's footing the bill for this, right? It's a joke. I'm joking. TRADITION! Welcome to the family!			
SHIFT	SHIFT	SHIFT	SHIFT	SHIFT	SHIFT	
	Jack (*enters with cigar*) Hey, who let all these handsome people in here? Huh?			Oh, hey, guys. Everyone, this is my dad, Jack.		
		(*Everyone	gets up	to shake	**Jack**'s hand.*)	

Woman 1	Man 1	Woman 2	Man 2	Woman 3	Man 3	Girl Boy
			Hey, Jack! Sam.			
	Great to meet you, Sam. Great to meet you.					
I'm Alice.						
	You must be Robbie's mother.				He's good, he's very good.	
(*Laughs.*) Grandmother, actually.	Get out! With that figure? (*Laughs.*)	Hi, Jack, I'm Nicole, Robbie's mom.				
Oh! (*Laughs.*)						
	An absolute pleasure. C'mere! (*He turns his handshake with **Nicole** into a sweet little twirl.*)	Whoa, ha ha!				
	Heck of a boy you raised.	Thank you.				
	If I may say one little thing to the love birds?	Of course.	Thanks Jack. Sure.			
	Now Steph and I went through a lot, what with everything between me and her mother, so forgive me for getting sentimental for a moment, but if I've learned anything, kids, it's this:					
	Love is not California. With love there's a lot of storms and hail and sleet. We all know something about sleet around here now don't we?					
	(*Knowing		laughs	at the	table.*)	

Woman 1	Man 1	Woman 2	Man 2	Woman 3	Man 3	Girl	Boy
	But you know what? It passes. It might not seem like it, but it passes and it makes everything else a hell of a lot more beautiful for having braved the stuff. So please, whatever you do –						
	Steph? Robbie? You hearing this? Whatever you do . . . don't move to California! It's very far away and I can't stand the place!						
	Okay, enough of that nonsense. Let's have a party!						
(*Laughs.*)		(*Laughs.*)	(*Laughs.*)	(*Laughs.*)	(*Laughs.*)		
				We won't, Daddy.	You got it, Jack.		
				(*And the family dances, stomping and a visceral celebration*	*dance, dance, hollering with a of love and life.*)		
		(**Sam** and **Nicky** look on with a kind of bewildered wonder, then begin to dance with one another. And just as quickly as the dance began it's over)					
SHIFT	SHIFT	SHIFT	SHIFT	SHIFT	SHIFT		
(*Sighs.*)	(*Sighs.*)	(*Sighs.*)	(*Sighs.*)	(*Sighs.*)	(*Sighs.*)		
		Oh, what an awesome wedding!	Can you believe this?		(*Drinks, stumbles a little.*)		
		Can you?					

Woman 1	Man 1	Woman 2	Man 2	Woman 3	Man 3	Girl	Boy
Where's Maddie run off to? I saw her with some man. Has anyone seen Maddie?			(*Castilian voice.*) Mmm, yes, yes, I can. (*They kiss.*)				
	God, she's beautiful. Isn't my little girl beautiful?						
My wedding night was something else, let me tell you. I had only been with one man before Robert – one! Oh, but thank God, thank God for that.							
				Kinda loud, honey.	(*Clinks a glass aggressively, stands. Drunk.*)		
					I want to thank my incredible family.		
					Mom: you're awesome. Dad: thanks. Thanks for everything I mean I know you don't, like, condone our marriage or anything but it's fine it's a little (*gesture*) but it's fine.		
			Stephanie, honey, you have to know I never said anything like that. I adore you. I totally adore you.	I never said that.			
				I think my husband's had a little too much fun. (*Takes the drink.*)	Hey!		
				What?	Give it back.		

Woman 1	Man 1	Woman 2	Man 2	Woman 3	Man 3	Girl	Boy
					I love you.		
				No way.			
		(*Pretty damn drunk.*) Have another drink, Steph!					
					So can I have it back now or what?		
				I love you too.			
		(*Drinks.*) You're not drinking? You just got married!		Oh I'm not drinking.			
				I know, but I really shouldn't.			
(*Pretty damn drunk.*) Oh, pull the cork out of your ass and drink up! (*Laughs.*)							
				Thanks, yeah, I would guys I would but I feel I feel a little sick. Oh . . .			
SHIFT	SHIFT	SHIFT	SHIFT	SHIFT	SHIFT	SHIFT	
					(*He clinks a glass.*)	**Jackie** (*enters*)	
					Hey, guys! Guys! Everyone! Hey! I wanna introduce you . . . to Jacquelyn.		
	Heeeeeey-oooo.						
Ooooooooh.		(*Laughs and claps.*)					
		Oh my God, she's gorgeous, she's – Oh, Robbie, Stephanie, she's perfect, she's just perfect.	That's my boy! (*Laughs.*)				
You must be very proud, Jack.	You're damn right.	Wow. Wow.			Isn't she?		

Woman 1	Man 1	Woman 2	Man 2	Woman 3	Man 3	Girl **Jackie**	Boy
				Say hello, Jackie.		Hello.	
	Oooh, would you look at her? Look at those cheeks.	Oooooooh.	Aaahhhhhhhhh. She's cute, she is very cute. You're a doll, Jackie. What a miracle.		Yeah, she's pretty much the best.		
	Who wants another Cadillac Margarita?! Yeah, I invented this motherfucker!						
	(*Laughs.*)	Ooooooh!				Hello!	
Aaaaaahhhh. (*Drunker.*) Picture time! Picture time!					Grandma.		
Oh shut up. Saaaay nacho!			Mom.				
	Nacho.	Nacho.	Nacho.	Nacho.	Nacho.	Nacho.	
SHIFT	SHIFT	SHIFT	SHIFT	SHIFT	SHIFT	SHIFT	
			(*He clinks a glass.*)				
			So I've heard a rumor, a teeny, tiny rumor that I'm . . . GONNA HAVE A GRANDSON!				
Ooooooh! A picture! We need to take a picture! Where's my camera? Has anyone seen my camera?	(*Whistle and applause.*)	What? Oh, that's incredible! That's so – !	A boy! A baby boy!	It's true, yeah, we're expecting again, yeah, yeah, isn't that great?	Yep, yep, thanks, ha ha. Yeah, sweetie?	Dad.	
						I'm gonna have a brother?	
Oh for the love of God, Jack	That's my Steph. That's my little Steph. Hey, lemme buy you a drink, Alice.	It's so great! When are you due? You've got to be thrilled.	Wow. WOW.	Pretty soon.	That's right.		
	(*Laughs.*)						

Woman 1	Man 1	Woman 2	Man 2	Woman 3	Man 3	Girl	Boy
	You're a spitfire, you know that?	I am, I am so happy for you.	Hey-oooooo! Ha ha ha ha!	I am, we both are, we're really excited. *She holds* **Robbie's** *hand.*	Yes, your brother's gonna be very nice.	Is he gonna be nice?	
					Of course.	Promise?	
							CLANG.
							(The boy enters and is served a plate of chicken fingers. The plate is heavy. It makes a big clang sound when it hits the table. Everyone stops what they're doing. They avoid eye contact. This will take the boy a long time to eat. He exits when he's finished.)
(Long pause.)	*(Long pause.)*	*(Long pause.)*	*(Long pause.)*	*(Long pause.)*	*(Long pause.)*	*(Long pause.)*	*(Long pause.)*
	Damn it.	I'm sorry.					
	Goddamn it.		Did they tell you what happened?		Dad. *(He drinks.)*		
		I'm so sorry.					
				(Sobs and runs off.)			

Woman 1

Alice

(*She is shaken, as if reliving her husband's death all over again.*)

When my husband died, I went to this man downtown, who worked in this little room with pastels on the walls, and I'd sit in a chair and talk to him. Only I don't remember myself talking; I only knew that I had talked because of the bill I got in the mail every month. And I wish I could remember what I said. I hope I didn't tell him anything terrible about your father, 'cause I loved him.

Yes, sometimes Robert was unkind to me, but at the core of him was a good person – one of the best people the world has ever known.

So what I've started doing is I've begun to write letters, and these letters are addressed to my husband, and I talk to him. I tell him how much I miss him, I tell him what's happening in your lives, and the baseball scores and the state of the yard, and I tell him how glad I'll be to see him.

And I've told him how he has a great-grandchild on his way to meet him, and how, though none of us ever met him, he is a very curious person, a very kind person, and they will have lots to talk about.

Oh, my husband will have lots to tell your son, so don't be sad.

Don't be sad.

I was sad for a long time, but if you just get a little envelope and talk to him, it'll make you feel so much better.

Why, just try now. Just try writing to him now. Just write right here, say hello.

Just say hello.

Tell him you love him right now, right this moment. Just say hello. Go on, go on, go on.

Woman 1	Man 1	Woman 2	Man 2	Woman 3	M 3	Girl	Boy
CLANG.							
(**Alice** *is served a big plate of food. She eats and eats. She exits when she's finished.*)							
(*Long pause.*)							
SHIFT	SHIFT	SHIFT	SHIFT	SHIFT			
		(*She takes* **Sam***'s hand.*)	(*He is deeply shaken. He stares blankly.*)	**Maddie** (*enters*) It's okay, Dad. It's gonna be okay.			
		We're so glad you made it, Maddie.		Thanks, Mom. Yeah, they let me take my finals early so –			
	She was a great woman. Of course, I didn't know her as long or as well as the rest of you but she was a real spitfire, and, sure, sure, well, who wants a drink?	Thank you, Jack. I'll take one.					
	That's the spirit! What'll you have?	Uh, how about a Cadillac Margarita? (*Laughs.*)	(*Smiles a little.*)				
	Alright! Now lemme track down that server.			Dad, if you need anything, seriously Dad.			
	(*Exits.*)						

W 1	Man 1	Woman 2	Man 2	W 3	Man 3	Girl	Boy
		Woman 2	**Man 2**		**Man 3**		
		I'm not going anywhere you understand me? I'm right here for you, Sam.			SHIFT		
					Robbie		
			You know, Mom used to say you never really understand how alone you are until you lose 'em both.		Hey sorry I can't be at the funeral, Dad. (Yeah I'll – Hang on, Dad. (Yeah, whiskey, thanks.) Dad, you there? (*Checks his watch.*) It's just my plane's about to leave for Orlando and – (Thanks thanks.) (*Drinks.*)		
		SHIFT	SHIFT		You there?		
		(*Exits.*)					
			Orlando? What's in Orlando?				
			Robbie				
			Hey look Dad, I gotta go.				
	Sam I'm here.						

Woman 1

SHIFT

(**Nicole** *alone. She waits, peruses the menu.*)

Nicole

There you are.

It's okay, Maddie, sit down.

It's not a problem.

So what's up?

What? Maddie, holy shit. Maddie.

With who?

I didn't, I didn't know you were seeing anyone. Darius?

A year? Okay, so what's, what's the story with Darius?

Man 1

. . . Orlando.

Yeah okay.

Well, lemme know if you change your mind, buddy.

Woman 2

SHIFT

Maddie

(*enters*)

Hey, Mom.

Sorry I'm late.

Thanks, um, thanks for meeting me. I know it's last minute –

(*She sits.*)

(*Hopeful.*) It's not, well, okay, um, I'm pregnant!

Yeah.

His name's Darius. It just, just sorta happened.

Yeah, for like a year now.

Well, he's a painter.

Man 2

I'd be there if I could.

It's just . . . too much.

(*Checks his watch.*) It's just a little too much. (*Drinks.*)

Woman 1   **M 1**   **Woman 2**   **M 2**   **W 3**   **M 3**   **Girl**   **Boy**

Woman 1: Wow.

Woman 2: He's really talented, Mom.

Woman 1: So I mean, is that it? Have you covered, I don't know, every genre? I mean there was that video artist, then there was that string of musicians, that dancer, that actor, you had that chiropractor for a while – not sure that counts as an artist, but –

Woman 2: Painting is not a genre, it's a form of visual –

Woman 2: Okay.

Woman 2: Okay, it's not like that, Mom.

Woman 1: Oh lighten up. When did you get so serious?

Woman 2: We're in love, Mom, okay? We're in love.

Woman 2: Uh, hello.

Woman 1: Maddie, honey, trust me. I used to fall for these types of guys all the time – these scrappy, needy, narcissistic . . .

Woman 2: Types? What types? Scrappy?

Woman 1: Oh, you know. I mean the guy I was dating before I met your father was –

Woman 2: Uh, no, I don't.

Woman 1: Well, he was a freak, but he was a sexy freak – extremely attentive – so I get it. I get the thing you're going through.

Woman 2: So now Darius is a freak?

Woman 2: Okay, you haven't even met him. I'm not going through anything. I'm in love.

Woman 1: Remember Steven? Jeremy? Uh, uh . . . Marcus?

Woman 2: Yeah, I've dated a bunch of guys – so what?

Woman 1: Are you and Dario –

Woman 2: Darius

Woman 1: Right. Are you and he planning to get married or – ?

Woman 2: Married?! Oh my god, who are you? You and Dad barely had a wedding!

Woman 1: Forget it. Forget I said anything.

Woman 1: (*Small pause.*)

Woman 2: (*Small pause.*)

Woman 1: Alright, well you know what? You get older and you start to see things a little differently.

Woman 1	Man 1	Woman 2	Man 2	W 3	M 3	Girl	Boy
		Okay, so now I have to be like Robbie and his perky little wife, and everyone else in this fucking wasteland. Yeah right.					
This isn't about Robbie.							
		That's a first. And for the record: that wedding sucked. It was super cheesy.					
Oh get over it.							
		Hey, why don't you get a drink?					
I stopped drinking							
		Oh, really?					
Yes.							
		When?					
When that alcoholic grandmother of yours finally kicked the bucket. (*Laughs.*)							
		(*Laughs.*)					
Wow, Maddie, another grandchild. Well, I'm – You know what? I'm ecstatic.							
		Really?					
Of course! You're my baby girl! Now come here! (*She hugs* **Maddie**.)							
		Thanks, Mom.					
. . . just don't fuck it up okay?							
SHIFT	SHIFT	SHIFT	SHIFT			SHIFT	
	Sam (*delighted*) You've gotta be kidding.	**Maddie** (*sings*) Happy, happy birthday from all of us to you.					
Nicole (*sings*) Happy, happy birthday from all of us to you.			**Robbie** (*sings*) Happy, happy birthday from all			**Jackie** (*sings*) Happy, happy birthday from all	

Woman 1	Man 1	Woman 2	Man 2	W 3 M 3 Girl	Boy
Happy, happy birthday, we're all so proud of you. Happy, happy birthday from all of us to you. Happy, happy birthday, may all your dreams come true. Happy birthday, SAAAAAAAM. (*Claps.*)		Happy, happy birthday, we're all so proud of you. Happy, happy birthday from all of us to you. Happy, happy birthday, may all your dreams come true. Happy birthday, SAAAAAAAM. (*Whistles.*)	Happy, happy birthday, we're all so proud of you. Happy, happy birthday from all of us to you. Happy, happy birthday, may all your dreams come true. Happy birthday, SAAAAAAAM. (*Claps.*)	Happy, happy birthday, we're all so proud of you. Happy, happy birthday from all of us to you. Happy, happy birthday, may all your dreams come true. Happy birthday, GRAAANDPAAA. (*Jumps a little.*)	
	(*Laughs. He might take a picture.*)	(*Everyone is in*	*a very jovial mood.*)		
	Now who hatched this little scheme?				
Jackie, how could you?!	Nicky?		I'm afraid that's classified information.	GRANDMA!	
I couldn't help myself. Happy birthday, Sam. (*She kisses him.*)		(*Hugs.*) Happy birthday, Dad. Dad –	(*Hugs.*) We love you, Dad.		
	(*Big smile.*) Well there's nothing that works up the appetite quite like a public seruhm, uh, serum . . . Oh, Nicky, what is that word?				
Serenade! (*Laughs.*)	(*Smiles.*)	(*Laughs.*)	(*Laughs.*)		
	Right right, serenade! So, uh, who wants an appetizer?		Bring it on.		

Woman 1	Man 1	Woman 2	W 3 M 3 Girl	Man 2	Boy
Uh, your daughter's pregnant, Sam.	How about calamari?				
Sam –	So? She's not allowed to eat calamari?	Dad –			
	I thought pregnant women ate everything.			Dad, it's a shellfish.	
	I've seen 'em at the aquarium and I don't buy it for a second.				
When have you ever been to an aquarium?					
				Well, I hate to break it to you, but science has a system, a classification system –	
	Robbie, it's cooked! How can it be bad for her if it's cooked?				
		It's okay, Dad, I'm just being careful.			
	(*Warm.*) There's being careful and then there's being crazypants, and I think you're being a little crazypants.				
				(*Drinks.*) Hey, it's tricky stuff. You know, Steph and I went through the same thing with –	
			Dad.		
			Daddy.		
			Hey, Daddy.		

Woman 1	Man 1	Woman 2	Man 2	W 3	M 3	Girl	Boy
			Hold on, Dad. What's up, Jackie?				Can I get a corn dog?
No way.			A corn dog?				
	Oh Nicole, let her have the corndog.						Yeah, they're the best.
Now Jackie, what do you think your mom'll say when she finds out we let you have a corndog?							
							Um . . . did you get me one?
(*Laughs.*) Somehow I don't think so.	(*Laughs.*) She's a doll. I always said she's a doll.	(*Laughs.*)	(*Laughs.*) No, no. Mommy will not be happy with Daddy if she comes back from her business trip and finds her little girl hopped up on preservatives. No, you'll get something else.			She would! Dad!	
						I'll only have a little, I promise!	
	So how's work, stranger?	Dad.	Uh, Steph's new venture's taking off so –				
	No, I mean your work –		You know, same old same old.				
		Uh, hello. Earth to Dad.					
	I'm talking to your brother.		(*Drinks.*)				

Woman 1	Man 1	Woman 2	Man 2	W 3	M 3	Girl	Boy
		Well I wanna give you a birthday present.					
	Can it wait?						
		No.					
	(*Closes his eyes. Opens his hands. Playful.*) Alright, lay it on me.						
		(*Takes his hand.*) I have decided to name him after you.						
	Who? What are you talking about?						
What do you think she's talking about, Sam?							
		Uh, him. My baby. Oh my God.					
	It's a boy?						
		Yeah.					
	And you're naming him after me?						
		Yes.					
	Well, hey, that's pretty cool! (*Laughs.*)						
SHIFT	SHIFT	SHIFT	SHIFT	SHIFT			SHIFT
							Sammy (*enters*) MEEERRRRY EX-MAS! MERRRRRRY EX-MAS! (*He does a hyperactive ninja move.*)
Well, look who it is!							
	Sammy's back!							

Woman 1	Man 1	Woman 2	Man 2	W 3 M 3 Girl	Boy
		Sammy, honey, sit down next to your cousin. The food's gonna be coming out soon.			
	(*Kinda racist accent.*) Hoooo. Beware the Sammy-rai!				
Very funny, Sam.	(*Laughs.*)				HO HO HO!
		A little racist, Dad.		Ow! Don't yell in my ear.	HI-YA!
				Dad, make him stop.	Fine.
		Sammy, how many times do I have to tell you? Leave your cousin alone.	Maddie? Your son, can you get him to –		
		Now say you're sorry.			Sorry, Jackie. (*He kisses her cheek.*)
				Ew! Don't!	
	(*Laughs.*)			You got my cheek wet.	
		Come on, Dad, you're just encouraging him.	Buddy –		What? I'm saying sorry!
	The kid's funny.				
	So what were you up to out there, (*racist*) Sammy-rai?				
		You what? No.			
					I was making a snowman ...WITH TITS.
Well, okay then.	(*Laughs.*)		(*Weird look.*)		
	Oh yeah? What size were her sno-cones? Huh?				Yeah!

Woman 1	Man 1	Woman 2	Man 2	W 3	M 3	Girl	Boy
Sam, grow up. He doesn't even know what he's saying.	(*Laughs.*) Come on, Nicky, it's a joke!						(*Laughs.*)
							Then a dog came over and peed on it, so it looked like the snowman peed while standing up, but girls don't pee standing up, only boys do. SO I PUNCHED HER TITS OFF!
All right. Where's he getting this stuff?		God, okay. No, don't. Don't do that again, okay? You have to be nice to girls, even snowman girls.	He's got an imagination, I'll give him that.				
							HI-YAH!
		Well, for starters, because your mother's a girl and you wanna be nice to me, don't you?					Why?
							Sometimes.
Hey!		Sammy!	You know, Mad, I know a guy, like a child-behavioral guy –				
		Thanks but no thanks, Rob.	Are you sure?				
							(*He does something ridiculous.*) YAH YAH YAH.

Woman 1	M 1	Woman 2	Man 2	W 3 M 3 Girl	Boy
					PREEEESENTS!
You know what! Let's do some presents!		I thought we weren't doing Christmas tonight.		You're loud in my ear again!	
Well, now we're doing Christmas.		Come on, guys. I didn't know this was happening. I haven't done my shopping.			
(*She tries to slow things down.*) Jackie, darling . . . since you have been so well behaved, you get to go first! (*Presents a box.*)				(*She opens it. Inside is a compass on a necklace.*) I don't know what it is.	
			It's a compass, honey. See, those are magnets and –	How's it do that?	
It can take you wherever you want to go.				And I can go anywhere with a compass?	
Yep! Anywhere! You can go anywhere!		(Sammy.)	It's a metaphor. Now what do you say to Grandma Nicky?		(Where's mine? Where's my present?!)
You're very welcome.		(Be patient.)		Thank you.	
				How do you turn it on?	(What? I wanna go next.)
It's always on. It doesn't need to turn on.				But how's it take me places?	

Woman 1	Man 1	Woman 2	Man 2	W 3 M 3 Girl	Boy
	Hey.			You're being rude!	SHUT UP, JACKIE!
				I am not!	Well, you're being a spoiled little brat.
		Whoa. Sammy.			That's what my mom says.
			Hold on. None of this. Hey –	Take it back.	
Now where the hell did he learn that?	Relax, Robbie. They're children.	No. No. I don't know where he got that.	What? Did you? Maddie, seriously? Did you tell him that?		
			(To Sam.) Let me handle it, Dad.		*TWAT TWAT TWAT!*
		Sammy! Oh my God. Get over here!	Say what? What did he say?	Daddy!	I heard you say it to Dad!
	The T word.				
		Nothing, he didn't – See? He didn't say anything			Nothing.
	(You know, maybe your sister could watch him next time we go out.)		They're cousins. He needs to learn to respect his cousin.		I was just making fun.
(My sister's not a babysitter, Sam.)	*(Can't hurt to ask.)*	I'm sorry, Rob, really. I don't know where he got that. *(She gives **Sammy** a look.)* *(Sternly whispers to her son.)* Shut ... up			*(**Sammy** grins at his mom, then hides it.)*

Woman 1	Man 1	Woman 2	Man 2	W 3 M 3 Girl	Boy
SHIFT	SHIFT	SHIFT	SHIFT	SHIFT SHIFT	SHIFT
And of course your father insisted on taking a picture of every damn thing we came across, every, uh, church, painting, conquistador . . .	Matador.	(*Smiles.*) Big surprise		(*Exits.*)	(*Exits.*)
What?	Conquistador's the soldier guy. The matador's the guy with the cape. Ho ho, toro! toro!				
All right. Whatever. You name it, Sam snapped it.	Pardon me for wanting to remember the things I've shared with the woman I love. (*Takes her hand.*)		(*Drinks.*) It sounds great, Mom. Sounds like Barcelona was really great.		
(*Smiles.*) Yeah, yeah . . . it was pretty fucking rad. (*Kisses* **Sam** *on the cheek.*)	(*Laughs.*)	(*Laughs.*)			
		Hey, guys, we're in public.	Well, there they are.	**Jackie** (*enters*) PEW PEW PUCKOOOO BAM BOOM EXPLOOOSION!	**Sammy** (*enters*) BOOM BOOM BANG BOOM BANG BOOM WWWW! POOOWWWWW

Woman 1	M 1	Woman 2	Man 2	W 3 M 3	Girl	Boy
					(They do a kiddish karate-	*move high-five.)*
			Jackie, cut it out.			
You know it was quieter when they were fighting.						BEWARE THE SAMMY-RAI.
					AND NIIINJACKIE!	
						YAH YAH YAH.
			Maddie, you think you can prevent your son from further corrupting my daughter?		YAH YAH YAH.	You ready for chair battle?
		Uh, yeah, Rob, sure. Jackie's an innocent. Sammy's a – Hey, no. Uh, los ninos, no way.			BRING IT. *(She scurries around.)*	CHAAAAIR BATTLE. *(He scurries around.)*
			Well, I'm gonna get another drink. Does anyone else want another drink?			
		(Gives a look.)				
			What? It's a holiday. This is what people do on a holiday.			
		Uh, wow, okay.				
			You know what, I've already got a wife, Mad.			
		Do you, Rob? 'Cause no one's seen her for a while.	Oh, so now I'm supposed to take relationship advice from you?			

Woman 1	Man 1	Woman 2	Man 2	Woman 3	Man 2	Girl	Boy
						(They start to	*chair battle.)*
						YAHHHH.	YAHHHH.
Who the hell gave them firecrackers?		Guys, hey, both of you, cut it out. Go back outside and play, huh?					But we're out of firecrackers! *(Bangs the table.)*
	Hey.	Too bad.				Yeah, we blew 'em all up! BANG! *(Bangs table.)*	BOOM! POW!
	It's the Fourth! That's what kids do on the Fourth!	You're going,	Jackie.			Yeah, what about our corn dogs?	What about my corn dog?
		We'll come find you when dinner's here, okay?	Lis:en to your aunt.			Dad?	
		Bye! Byeeeee!				BEEEEEEOOOO – SHAPOOOM – *(She runs after him.)*	SHAPOOOM – *(He runs off.)*
SHIFT	SHIFT	SHIFT	SHIFT			SHIFT	SHIFT
You're telling me.		God, it's just, they grow up so fast.	Speak of the devil. *(Drinks.)* It's okay, honey. Have a seat.	**Jackie** *(enters.)* Hi, Daddy. Sorry we're late. *(kisses his cheek.)*	**Sammy** *(enters)* Mom. Hey, Mom. Mom. Mom. Hey, Mom.		

Woman 1	Man 1	Woman 2	Man 2	Woman 3	Man 3	Girl	Boy
		What is it, Sammy? I'm talking. You're interrupting me. Why are you always interrupting me?			I'm just letting you know I'm gonna be out past curfew. You told me to tell you if I was gonna be out past curfew so here I am telling you . . .Jeez.		
					You're such a spaz.		
	Hoo, big plans tonight, (*a little racist*) Sammy-rai?	Fine.					
	(*Laughs.*)				(*A little racist.*) Hooooo with your blessings, Grandpa Sam-sei. (*Laughs.*)		
			(*Weird look.*)				
			(*He stands. Raises his glass. He may chime it a little too aggressively. Drunk.*) Hey! Hello! In honor of Turkey Day, in the spirit of giving thanks, I would like to share what I am thankful for.				
		A little loud, Rob, a little –					
		Sammy.			(*Snickers.*) Booze.		
Go ahead					What?		

W 1	Man 1	Woman 2	Man 2	W 3	Man 3	Girl	Boy
			(*Holding it together.*)				
			Okay, well, uh, my family. I am so very thankful for my incredible family.				
					(*Snickers.*)		
			Excuse me?				
					You're excused.		
			Do you have something to say?				
					(*Gives a look.*)		
			Uh, (*Tries to laugh it off.*) now where was I?				
					Orlando.		
			What?				
					Uh, aren't you always in Orlando instead of with your incredible family? (*Laughs.*)		
		Sammy.					
					Hey, whoa.		
		Hey, Robbie, this is my son.					
					(*Laughs.*)		
			(**Robbie** *nearly explodes.*)				
			Okay, listen to me, you ungrateful little shit. Your mother might not be interested in disciplining you, but that doesn't mean you get to do or say whatever you want. You have to learn some respect. You have to learn a little decorum.				
					Like anyone knows what that means.		
	Hey, hold on.						
			This is your family, and you need to show them the love and patience they show you. No, no. You keep my wife out of this.				
					Oh, hey, speaking of family, where's Aunt Steph? Yeah, hey, Jackie, where's your mom? What, does she not like hanging out with us anymore? Are		

Woman 1	Man 1	Woman 2	Man 2	Woman 3	Man 3	Girl	Boy
	Look, guys, it's Thanksgiving				we not all perky enough for her or something?		
					I'm just asking a question.		
				Grow up, Sammy.	Grow some tits, Jackie.		
		This is unacceptable, absolutely unacceptable –	*(He grabs **Sammy** by the arm.)*		Whoa. *(Laughs.)* People are looking. I mean, you are totally embarrassing yourself.		
He's drunk. You're drunk.			*(Quiet.)* How dare you.				
			*(He lets go of **Sammy**'s arm.)* You know, it's no wonder your father left.	Dad, come on. He's just being a brat.	Seriously? Is that supposed to hurt my feelings?		
		Jesus Christ, Rob.	Look at what you're doing to your mother.		Me? Oh my God, you are so plastic.		
		Hey.					
		Hey.	You think this has been easy on her?				
		Leave him alone.			Yeah, leave me alone.		
		*(To **Sammy**.)* Don't you dare say another word.	God, Maddie, you have no idea how to handle anything, do you?				
				(There are people watching.)	*(Zip-the-lip motion.)*		

Woman 1	Man 1	Woman 2	Man 2	W 3	Man 3	Girl	Boy
Maybe Sammy should stay with Darius for a while.	Now, I'm not sure that's such a good idea.	No! No!	I'm just trying to help.				
Maddie, honey, I mean it. It might be for the best.		I don't need you. No. I can handle this myself!					
		I don't need help.					
		I'm not some damsel in distress. I am a grown woman! I don't care if you like the way I live my life. It's my life, okay? IT IS MY LIFE!					
		Ow. (*She feels under her armpit*).					
		(*A suspended*	*moment.*)				
		Why's it so hard?	Are you okay?				
Maybe you should see a doctor.		Why's it feel so hard?	It's gonna be okay.				
			Maddie, look at me. Hey, it's all gonna be okay.				
We're right here.		I'm sorry, Robbie.	No, hey, hey, just look at me.				
		Mom. Dad.	Look at me.				
		(*She turns to her son.*) Sammy . . .					
		Oh Oh!					Mom?
		CLANG.					
		(*She is served a giant, heavy plate of hot food. She eats and eats. She exits when finished.*)					

Woman 1	Man 1	W 2	Man 2	Woman 3	Man 3	Girl	Boy
SHIFT	SHIFT	SHIFT	SHIFT	SHIFT	SHIFT		
					Mom? Mom?		
(*Shattered.*) Maddie . . .	(*Shattered.*) (*He takes* **Nicole***'s hand.*)		(*Deeply shaken.*) No. God. No.				
	I . . . I never . . .		Maddie.		No. No. Mom.		
Sammy, here. Come here, darling.				I'm right here, Sammy, seriously, if you need anything.			
Sammy.					No. No. Mom.		
Honey, come here –							
Sammy, please –					No, no, no, no.		
(*She beckons the family to hold hands. They do.* **Nicole** *leads them in prayer.*)							
Our Father, who art in heaven, hallowed be thy name. Thy kingdom come, thy will be done, on earth as it is in heaven.	Our Father, who art in heaven, hallowed be thy name. Thy kingdom come, thy will be done, on earth as it is in heaven.		Our Father, who art in heaven, hallowed be thy name. Thy kingdom come, thy will be done, on earth as it is in heaven.	Our Father, who art in heaven, hallowed be thy name. Thy kingdom come, thy will be done, on earth as it is in heaven.	(*He very noticeably does not pray.*)	Our Father, who art in heaven, hallowed be thy name. Thy kingdom come, thy will be done, on earth as it is in heaven.	Our Father, who art in heaven, hallowed be thy name. Thy kingdom come, thy will be done, on earth as it is in heaven.

Woman 1	Man 1	W 2	Man 2	Woman 3	Man 3	Girl	Boy
Give us this day our daily bread, and forgive us our trespasses, as we forgive those who –	Give us this day our daily bread, and forgive us our trespasses, as we forgive those who –		Give us this day our daily bread, and forgive us our trespasses, as we forgive those who –	Give us this day our daily bread, and forgive us our trespasses, as we forgive those who –	You know what? You know what! You know what!	You know what? Give us this day our daily bread, and forgive us our trespasses, as we forgive those who –	Give us this day our daily bread, and forgive us our trespasses, as we forgive those who –
					(He stands. He berates the rest.)		
					You didn't care about her. None of you cared.		
			Sammy, buddy –		No, just shut up! She was my mom, okay? She was my mom and and none of you gave a shit.		
					You could have, like, tried to raise money or, like, given up your jobs to be with her. You could have, like, stopped your lives.		

| W 1 | M 1 | W 2 | M 2 | W 3 | Man 3 | Girl | Boy |

Man 3

Is it so hard to, like, stop your life for just like a second?

It's like everyone goes back to their lives so quickly they barely take a breath before it's like, back to normal.

We should take the time, you know, we should take the time to, like, not be assholes. You're all just a bunch of assholes!

This whole, this whole country is just a bunch of fuckin' assholes! Everyone's just sitting around and talking and not doing a fuckin' thing about all the hurt and pain and, like, bad shit that's going down all over the world, and I'm tired of just sitting here and talking. I wanna go out there and do something about it, I wanna go out there and do something about it – and if that means I have to, like, sign up and kill a few people, kill a few assholes to do it, then fine. Then I'll go sign up and kill a few assholes so people will understand that it doesn't have to be like this.

We can be better and I'm gonna show you, I'm gonna show all of you assholes.

She was my mother, so stop looking at me like that.
I'm going, okay?
I don't care what you say, I'm gonna make a difference.

'Cause I'm sick of it, I'm so sick of it I just want it to be different. That's it. I just want it to all be different.

CLANG.

(He is served a big plate of food. He eats and eats. Everyone averts their eyes. There's nothing to say really. He exits.)

(LONG, LONG, LONG PAUSE.)

Woman 1	Man 1
(**Sam** *and* **Nicole** *are left alone. Everything begins to move much, much slower now.*)	
SHIFT	SHIFT
(*She wears a tiny yellow ribbon.*)	
	(*Pause.*)
	What are you thinking of getting?
I don't know, Sam.	
	(*Pause.*)
	These menus keep getting bigger and bigger.
Mm.	
(*Pause.*)	(*Pause.*)
Robbie called.	Oh, yeah? What'd he say?
Not much. He was at one of Steph's conferences.	
(*Pause.*)	(*Pause.*)
She got some kind of award at her high school.	How's Jackie?
	(*Pause.*)
What pictures?	Did he mention the pictures?
	From their visit.
Oh, no. Why would they, Sam?	I thought he'd say.
Well he didn't.	
(*Pause.*)	(*Pause.*)
What?	Hm?
(*She shakes her head.*)	Did you say something?
	I think I might get the salmon.

Woman 1	Man 1
SHIFT	SHIFT
(*Pause.*)	(*Pause.*)
Robbie called.	When?
This morning.	
(*Pause.*)	(*Pause.*)
What?	Nicole.
You were asleep.	Why didn't you tell me?
I called to you.	I was not.
(*Pause.*)	(*Pause.*)
He's got a new job.	Well, what'd he say?
He hasn't started yet.	Oh yeah? Does he like it?
(*Pause.*)	(*Pause.*)
She's fine.	How's Jackie?
I don't know, Sam.	Did she get our present?
SHIFT	SHIFT
(*The yellow ribbon is now gone.*)	
(*Pause.*)	(*Pause.*)
My sister?	Hey how's your sister?
She's . . . she's gone, Sam. You know this.	Yeah – she still in restaurants?
(*Pause.*)	(*Pause.*)

Woman 1	Man 1	W 2	Man 2	W 3	M 3	Girl	Boy
(*Smiles at Sam. Takes his hand.*) Why don't we order? (*Pause.*) SHIFT	Then who's gonna watch the kids?						
	(*Pause.*) SHIFT	SHIFT					
			Robbie (*enters*) Sorry I'm late.				
			How are you?				
			Hi, Mom. (*Kisses her cheek.*) Dad. Uh, happy anniversary . . . what a run, huh?				
	Whoa, ho ho! Robbie!		(*He adjusts his watch. Smiles.*) You know how it is. Can I get you guys something to drink?				
We're good. We're just so happy to see you.							
	How long are you staying?						
			(*Drinks.*)				
I'm fine.	Well, we'll make the most of it, won't we? Where's, uh, where's Jackie?		She's, uh, backpacking with her friends in Norway, then Iceland next week.				
Wow, exotic.	I hear they eat whale there. Now don't tell me that's a shellfish! (*Laughs.*) Whoa, ho ho!		Uh huh.				
It's very exciting.	Big change of scenery from Massachusetts. Are you sure?		Connecticut, Dad. She goes to school in Connecticut.				

Woman 1	Man 1	W 2	Man 2	Woman 3	M 3	Girl	Boy
(Pause.) Have you heard from Steph?			Yeah, I write the checks, so – *(Pause.)*				
			(Bristles.) Mom, please. *(Drinks.)*				
SHIFT	SHIFT	SHIFT	SHIFT	SHIFT			
				Jackie *(enters, wearing her compass necklace)* Hey. Hi.			
	Whoa ho ho!						
Jackie! Oh, darling! Look at you all grown up! My God! You're so beautiful!							
				Thanks.			
And you're wearing the necklace I gave you! How wonderful!							
	Well, have a seat.						
				This ? Oh yeah, huh.			
				Oh, sorry, I can't stay. My boyfriend's plane just got in, and he lost his luggage so he's – *(Gestures.)*			
	At least have some coffee, Maddie, or –						
			Dad.				
	What?						
			This is Jacquelyn.				
	Of course it is! What'd I say?						
You said Maddie.							

Woman 1	Man 1	W 2	Man 2	M 3	Girl	Boy	Woman 3
	So? What's wrong with that?						
							Shit, I'm already late. Sorry – it's so nice to see you guys.
							(She leaves.)
Sam.	Now Madeleine . . .		Dad.				
Sam.	I'll say what I want. Leave me alone! Lemme be. Lemme be. Uh, what –		Dad.				
Here, let me – Here. Sh. *(She tucks a napkin into **Sam**'s shirt.)*	What, what, uh, don't touch me! I can . . . don't . . . Leave me alone. I don't want you touching me.						
	(Nicole *feeds* **Sam.** *She takes her time.)*		*(He watches this for a long while.)* So, look. I know this is bad timing, Mom, but uh – *(He stands. Finishes his drink.)* Hey, let me pay for this, okay? That helps right? If I pay?				
When are you coming back?			I don't know. *(He adjusts his watch.)* Things are pretty crazy, what with the lay-off, and uh, well, I met this woman, this amazing woman. Maddie would've . . . . . . Maddie would've loved her.				

Woman 1	Man 1	W 2	Man 2	W 3	M 3	Girl	Boy
			She's got a lotta spunk, and uh, kids. And they're great kids, a great family, so . . .				
That's wonderful.			It's all a little too much right now, but you should really come out and visit sometime. It's nice –				
I'm sure it is.			Well . . . hey . . . soon, okay? I'll be home again soon. I love you.				
(Long pause.) *(The pace slows down considerably.* **Nicole** *continues to feed* **Sam**.*)* My God, where does the time go?			*(He kisses* **Nicole***. Turns to his father. With regret . . .)* Bye Dad. *(He leaves.)*				
(A little laugh to herself.) Where does it all go? Oh, Sam. I will never forget the day we . . . the day we . . . I will never . . . ever . . .	**(Sam** *begins to eat by himself.)*						
Oh, Sam. Sam, my Sam. *(She watches him eat.)* Sam, Sam, Sam.	*(And* **Sam** *slowly recedes from view.)* *(Long pause.)*						
(Long pause.)							
SHIFT							SHIFT

SHIFT

Woman 1	M 1	Woman 2	M 2	W 2	M 3	Girl	Boy
		Jackie					**Matthew**
		(*enters wearing necklace*)					(*enters*)
		Grandma?					
Is that . . . Is that Jackie?		Hey, grandma.					
My God, look at you, Jackie. You look just like your mother.		(*Smiles.*) Yeah, thanks.					
It's been so long. How are you?		I'm good. I'm, well – I want you to meet someone. This is Matthew. Matthew, this is your great-grandmother, Nicole. She gave me this when I was little like you. (*Gestures to necklace.*)					
							Hi.
He's precious.							
(*She touches the boy's hair.*)							
Oh! A great-grandchild! My God! To see the day!							
(*She is upset.*)							
We started something, didn't we?							
We really started something.							
		Are you okay? Grandma?					
(*She stares off.*)		Hey why don't we eat, huh? Grandma? Oh now, where – Where's that server?					
							She's probably hiding from you, Mom.

W 1 M 1 Woman 2   **M 2 W 3 M 3 Girl Boy**

Oh yeah? Why's that?

'Cause she's playing a trick on you?

And what kind of trick might that be?

A funny trick.

Funny how?

Funny like a surprise.

Oh yeah?

Yeah, she's maybe hiding on a shelf in the kitchen while you're, like, "Where is she?" "When's she gonna get here?" until you think about it so much that you forget, and once you forget she's gonna sneak up on you when you're not thinking about it in her special server sneaking shoes.

Really slowly, sneak, sneak, sneak, sneak.

Then what?

Mnm. Then she's gonna take your order.

And what am I gonna order?

Mmmm, everything.

Everything?

Yeah, 'cause it's been so long and you're so hungry that when you finally get the chance to order you're gonna get everything on the menu.

That's a lot.

Well, it seems like a lot, but when you really think about it's not so much.

Yeah, I guess not. I think you might be right.

I know I'm right.

I love you.

You don't have to get cheesy, Mom.

(Cheesy voice.) I love you so much.

(Laughs.) Mom.

Now say goodbye.

Bye, Grandma Steph.

No, honey. Steph's my mom like I'm your mom. This is my grandma Nicky, like grandma Steph's your grandma.

Woman 1	M 1 Woman 2	M 3 W 3 M 3 Girl	Boy
			It's a lot to remember.
	That's okay. Say goodbye.		Goodbye, lady.
	(*Laughs.*) Goodbye, lady.		(*He begins to recede from view.*)
	(*She begins to recede from view.*)		Goodbye, lady.
	Goodbye, lady.		
	Goodbye, lady.		(*Fainter and fainter.*)
	(*Fainter and fainter.*)		Goodbye, lady.
	Goodbye, lady.		Goodbye, lady.
	Goodbye, lady.		Goodbye, lady.
	. . . Goodbye		(*He's faded away . . .*)
	(*She's faded away . . .*)		

(*But **Nicole** remains. The table is hers and hers alone. She waits and waits and waits. But the wait is*

so,

so

long . . .)

Lampedusa

Anders Lustgarten

Lampedusa was first performed at the Soho Theatre, London, on 8 April 2015 before transferring to the HighTide Festival, Aldeburgh, on 10 September 2015 in a HighTide and Soho Theatre co-production. It featured the following cast and creative team:

Stefano	Ferdy Roberts
Denise	Louise Mai Newberry

Director	Steven Atkinson
Designer	Lucy Osborne
Lighting designer	Elliot Griggs
Sound designer	Isobel Waller-Bridge

Spotlight on **Stefano**, *alone, reflective. He stares out into the great wide expanse of the Mediterranean Sea.*

Stefano   This is where the world began. This was Caesar's highway. Hannibal's road to glory. These were the trading routes of the Phoenicians and the Carthaginians, the Ottomans and the Byzantines. If you look carefully, my grandfather used to say, you can still make out the wakes of their ships. Our favourite food is *bottarga*, salted roe: it tastes like being slapped in the face by a wave you didn't see coming. We all come from the sea and back to the sea we will go. The Mediterranean gave birth to the world.

On a clear day I am Caesar. The prow of the boat cuts the horizon in two. Sunlight shatters off the waves. Dolphins. Great flocks of seabirds. The ocean sucks and pulses like a giant lung, breathing life into the world even as the wind pushes the air from my lungs and makes it hard to breathe. I forget this is a job. I forget why I am here, except to be alive.

And then I see. And I remember why.

The lung has little black spots floating on its surface. Distant. Hardly visible in the light.

The boat gets closer.
Salvatore cuts the engine.
We drift alongside . . .

Beat.

The bodies of the drowned are more varied than you'd think. Some are warped, rotted, bloated to three times their natural size, twisted into fantastical and disgusting shapes like the curse in that story my grandmother used to tell me. Dead of winter, chills down yer spine.

Others are calm, no signs of struggle, as if they're dozing in the sun on a lazy summer afternoon and a tap on the arm will bring them gently awake. Those are the hardest. Because they're the most human.

They're overwhelmingly young, the dead. Twenties. Thirty at most.

Kids, a lot of them.

You have to be to make the journey, I suppose.

It feels very strange to see so many young people dead. Unnatural.

Everybody tries, at one time or another, to wake the ones that still look human.

A pinch. A splash of water on the face.

'Come on, get up.'

Beat.

The state of a drowned corpse depends on several factors.

How long it's been in the water.

Temperature.

Tides. If the tides bring colder water up from the depths, bodies can be preserved more or less intact for a surprisingly long time.

That has two consequences. One is that although the cold water preserves the bodies, it also alters the make-up of human flesh. Physically, chemically, whatever, I don't know exactly, but . . .

They fall apart in your hands. If they've been in the drink a while. Slide apart and fall to pieces. The sensation is like . . . like oiled lumpy rubbish bags sliding through your fingers.

The other is that colder water brings more fish. The drowned lie facedown, heads lolling down into the water, and fish go for the easiest parts to reach.

Eyelids.

Pieces of the face.

Fingertips.

Anything not protected by clothing, basically.

The bulging eyes of the dead. That's how you know they're gone.

The shock, the sheer horror, wears off eventually, but the sense of dread as we pull up, of not knowing what we're going to find? That never goes away.

Lights down on **Stefano**. *Lights up on* **Denise**, *mixed white and East Asian, cautious, observant. She watches us. Beat.*

Denise   There's all kinds of reactions. There's the ones who act like it's nowt. 'Can you come back later, love? I'm watching the telly.' 'A television means you have assets and therefore means of repayment, am I correct in that, sir?' They look at you different then. There's them who pretend not to understand English, so we have to use sign language. (*She rubs her fingers together and holds out a hand*) There's the ones who do a runner. I had a bloke jump out t'window on me the other day, not sure he remembered he were on the third floor. Broke his ankle in two places. When I caught up with him, hobbling across the car park, he goes, 'Oh, there you are, love. Left me chequebook in the car.'

And then there's the creative ones. Generally I find the madder the excuses, the more likely they are to be true. Today I had, 'I can't deal with this now, me python's just eaten me dog.' Went in after the bloke and fuck me if there isn't a *massive* snake lying across the carpet, in a right food coma, and bang in his middle is a dog-shaped bulge so tight you can actually make out the curls of the poor bugger's fur. 'That's a miniature Schnauzer, ent it?' I said to him. 'Lovely dogs. Full of energy.' He went *mad*.

All kinds of reactions.
But the overriding one is people do not take it seriously.
As if it's not really happening.
Not here. To them. Now.

People are strange.
When you're a stranger.

Beat.

It's a myth that we send the heavies round at the drop of a hat. There's a range of options available to us. First of all we put what's called a CPA, a Continuous Payment Authority, on the bank account. That gives us the right to access income streams ahead of other claimants, rent and such. After that it's calls to the house, to the employer (should there be one), letters. When none of that works, a more direct approach is required. That is where I come in.

The company prefers to send a woman. They think it leads to less violence. Two flaws with that theory. One is that men do not like to be embarrassed by a woman, and they particularly don't like being asked for money. It hurts their pride. So there are incidents.

The other is that half our customers are women. And the dirty little secret of women is women fucking hate each other. I've never been afraid collecting off a man, but I dread dealing with a woman.
Nails down yer cheek.
Spitting.
The nastiest, most malicious abuse about me race, me face, me body.

They judge me doing this job the way they'd *never* judge a man. Like I've violated some code of 'solidarity' they never let me in on in't first place. Girls who did slitty eyes at me in science class, who've put on four stone since, asking how I can live with meself.

I tell 'em: this is what working-class jobs used to be. Flexible, paid overtime. We're a growth industry: us, and prisons. Not my fault you ant kept up with modernity.

The ones that proper piss me off are them who make out they're fighting The Man by spunking someone else's money on a massive flat screen TV. This one sack of lard, clearly spent the entire loan on KFC cos she were visible from space. She kept going on about how I were a 'traitor to the working class.' Normally I try to stay, what's the word? Dispassionate. Keep a professional distance.
But this one deserved a little something.

So as we were serving the papers, I leant in and said, 'What d'you know about working class? You've never had either in your life.'
That shut her up.

The bottom line is: if you can't afford to pay a loan back, don't take one out.
Don't stand there quoting me figures, 'I only took out this much and you lot want three times as much back.'
Yes, thank you, Stephen Hawking, I can do the maths as well, the interest rate is down there in black and white.

Learn some discipline. If you ant got the money, do without.

I have. I *do*.

Lights down on **Denise**. *Lights back on* **Stefano**.

Stefano   My father was a fisherman. And his father before him. And before and before. I always thought, always knew, I'd make my living at sea.

But the fish are gone. The Med is dead.
And my job is to fish out a very different harvest.

Three years without work. Three years of pleading and queuing and niggly little bribes to a man who says he can help. And you sit, and you wait, and nothing happens, and you go back to him and he looks at you and shrugs and laughs a wheezy smoky laugh, and he doesn't give you your bribe back.

And you start again, your aims sinking slow like a pinholed boat. Turned down for stuff you turned your nose up at before. Borrowing money from my dad. Chiara's mum, who she doesn't get on with at the best of times.

And finally this. The job no-one else will take.

Beat.

I fucking wish they'd stop coming.

Not in the way Salvatore does.

Salvo's problem is he's an idealist. He joined to rescue people. To 'help'.

Those people are always the most selfish because it's to help on their terms.

And rescuing people is not the key part of the job. The key to the job is the dead. And Salvo began very quickly to hate these dead people, because they kept coming and coming and they wouldn't stop.

He began to take it personally, like they were dying just to upset him, to make him feel like a failure.

And now he calls them 'the niggers' and is going to vote Berlusconi in the next election.

Ridiculous.

For one thing, Berlusconi is banned from the next election. Read the papers, you twat.

And for another, because they aren't.

Only.

Black.

Syrians are the latest thing. Palestinians last summer when Gaza got bombed.

Egyptians and Libyans the past couple of years. We read the papers and we see a disaster, a crackdown, a famine, and we say: 'They'll be here next.'

Makes me laugh when people call them 'economic migrants'. It's like an earthquake – you feel the tremors far away and you know the tidal wave is coming.

My beef is, why us?

This is a small island. The refugee centre is swamped, twelve hundred in a place built for two or three. People sprawled on blankets in the street, kids playing in the dust behind barbed wire. It's embarrassing. Looks like Guantanamo.

We're a hospitable people but where else can we put 'em?

And then a chicken goes missing or some washing off a line, and there's shouting and we're the ones who look ignorant and small-minded, but where is everybody else? Why are we, a little dusty island you've never ever heard of, left to deal with all this alone?

And do the migrants not understand Europe is fucked? And Italy is double-fucked? And the south of Italy is triple-fucked? My younger brother, much smarter than me, degree in biochemistry (I think), and he had to go to London to find work. . . as a chef. He says the sous-chef is a biologist from Spain and the kitchen porter is a geneticist from Greece, and in their free time between courses they work on a cure for cancer.

That's a joke.
They don't get any free time.

Beat.

In Italy there's no hope. Everything is corrupt, the middle-aged cling grimly to their jobs and suffocate the rest of us, and nobody has any idea how to fix it. Pessimism is our national sport, you can see it in our football.

And these people, the survivors, the lucky ones, they come on land with these shining, gleaming eyes. And I resent them for it. I'll be honest, I do.

I resent them for their hope.

Lights down on **Stefano***. Lights up on* **Denise** *holding an essay.*

Denise   Here's summat I found out the other day: nine out of the ten poorest regions in Northern Europe, in comparative terms, are in 'Great' Britain.

Here's where they are:
West Wales
Cornwall
Tees Valley
Lincolnshire
The Independent Republic of South Yorkshire
Shropshire/Staffordshire
Lancashire

Northern Ireland
That's the top eight. Ninth is some wankstain in Belgium.
Tenth is East Yorkshire.

We also have one entry in the list of the ten richest areas.
It's the top entry, as it happens.
Can you guess where it is? I bet you'll never guess.
Inner London.

Put all that in me politics essay. Got the grade today, C+.
'Too on the nose. A lack of balance.' These are government
figures. Nobody else had them figures in their work, I
checked. The prospectus for this university claims to
encourage original thinking.
Do you want the truth or don't yer?

I was spat at on the bus this morning.
Couple of public schoolboys, I'd say.
I'd not heard 'chinky cunt' and 'fucking migrant' in that
accent until recently. But lately I get it quite a bit. Middle-
class people think racism is free speech now. All those twats
in their 'Je suis Charlie' T-shirts.

Summat about the Chinese an all. We're the last ones it's OK
to hate. The last who you can take the piss out of to us faces,
cos we'll do nowt back and all we're good for is DVD sellers
and takeaway owners and whores. You can say stuff to the
Chinese you wouldn't even say to Muslims. And I'm not even
a proper one. Don't fit in anywhere, me. Mixed and mouthy
and poor.

Beat.

The hatred in this country now.
The hatred and the bitterness and the rage. The misplaced,
thick, ignorant rage.
Blaming 'fucking migrants' for every single thing we don't
like about ourselves.

Four o'clock this afternoon, soaked to the skin, I'd been up
and down more piss-stained staircases than a Channel 4

benefits documentary, and I bang on the door and yet
another snide little prick yawned in me face, kicked aside a
knee-high pile of takeaway cartons and swore at me when I
asked him to pay, like I was the one in the wrong. And he
did not have a Syrian or a Romanian or a Ugandan accent,
let me tell you that.

You want to blame anyone for the state of this country, blame
people like him – all the lazy bastards. I do, that's why I
voted Tory. But don't blame the migrants.

Migrants don't scrape together their life savings, leave their
loved ones behind, bribe and fight and struggle their way
onto the undercarriage of a train or into a tiny hidden
compartment of a lorry with forty other people, watch their
mates die or get raped, all for the express purpose of
blagging sixty-seven-pound forty-six pence a week off of
Kirklees District Council.
People just don't act like that.
And if you need to believe they do, what does that say about
you?

Beat.

It don't matter.
What anybody says.
How many times me bloody mother tells me I'm too thick to
pass.

I am going to murder these exams.
I'm going to Oscar them, as I like to call it. As in Pistorius.
And if the results are good enough, I can go anywhere.
Australia. America.
China even. Doing well, ent they? That'd be fucking ironic.

Anywhere but here.

Slam the door on this washed-up country, turn me back, be
free. I don't know what free is, where I'll find it, but that is
where am I going and nobody will stop me.

Lights down on **Denise**. *Lights up on* **Stefano**.

Stefano   Dawn. Beautiful morning, not a whisper on the water, the rocks dusted with peach and apricot. The breeze like a sigh of happiness.

And the boat won't start.

Not a soul around to help. Salvo and I fiddle with the engine for half an hour, no joy. We're on the point of chucking it in, when one of the mounds of rags piled up on the pier starts to stir and yawn.

Stocky, wine-dark skin.

Nigerian, my guess.

I've got decent at telling the difference between Eritreans, Somalis, Senegalese. I take a bit of pride in it, as it goes. We have bets on who's what and I've won a few drinks off it.

What?

He watches us struggling and cursing for a while, this lad, with a look of amusement on his face. Doesn't do anything to help. In the end Salvo storms off, lobs a few choice words in the fella's direction. Short pause, he gets up. I'm thinking he's gonna wake up his mates to come and watch.

And then he fixes the boat.

Five minutes, it took him. 'Easy for me,' he says, grinning.

Modibo. From Mali.

A mechanic.

Not much use for a boat mechanic in the Sahara, I tell him.

'Yes! This is why Europe needs me! Boats, cars, planes, all I can do!' he goes, massive smile all over his face.

'You want drink coffee?'

You want me to buy you a coffee?!

'No, I buy for you!' Big laugh this time.

I'm off to work, mate.

He offers to get in the boat with me in case it packs up again.

No thanks. Chirpy fucker.

Beat.

You have to keep them at arm's length. If you let them get close, you never know what they might ask for. On the boat the survivors start talking to me, pleading their case, like I can do anything for them.

It's not part of my job to have to listen to their stories.
There's too many of them.
And it makes you think.
About the randomness of I get to walk these streets and he doesn't.
You start thinking about things like that, the ground becomes ocean under your feet.

And what if he does get in and we break down and he fixes it again and the bosses hear? That he can do stuff I can't do, for half the rate? You have to think about these things now. Here, in Europe, 2016. You have to watch yer back from every angle.

Beat.

So I thank the fella, shake his hand, bell Salvo and away we go. He waves to us as we head off, like a big gormless lump. I think that's the end of it.
Except the mad bastard clearly hasn't got the memo that we aren't gonna be mates, cos I keep running into him and he keeps being nice to me.
His big guileless face, open smile. What's he got to be so happy about? Keeps on offering to buy me an espresso, like he's made of money.
Be rude to say no.
Salvo sees us in the café, gives me a look, mutters something about 'soft touch'. He's paying, you gobshite!

Speaks shit Italian, Modibo. I say, why come somewhere you don't speak the language? He says I didn't come here, I came to Europe, the language of Europe is English.
Then he says something to me in English. I didn't understand it.
I tell him *vaffanculo*. He understands that alright.
See? Your Italian's improving already.

And then he plays me something. A song called
'Lampedusa'. It's meant to be about all the people who've
come here seeking a better life.
The drowning and the terror.
The hope and the futures.
I don't know if I can hear all that in there personally, but it's
beautiful. Listen.

'Lampedusa' by Toumani Diabaté and Sidiki Diabaté plays.

His village was burned down twice. Once by the military
because they said it was a stronghold of Islamic
fundamentalists, and once by Islamic fundamentalists
because they said it was a stronghold of the military.
The second time, they gave them an hour to get out, said
they'd kill anyone left behind. He stashed his family and
headed here. To earn the money to start afresh.

I mean, this is his story, God knows how much of it is true.
He could be making it all up.

Mali. Exotic.

Beat. The music fades. Lights down on **Stefano**. *Lights up on*
Denise.

Denise   You know ATOS? Course you do. They do them
Work Capability Assessments, where they go to morgues,
plane crashes, outbreaks of bubonic plague, and tell people
they'll be fine, it's just a head cold, and by the way their
benefits have been stopped. Me mum got the dreaded ATOS
call today.

Mum's been called a lot of things over the years. She's gone
from 'retarded' to 'slow' to 'disabled' to 'differently abled'.
Which makes it sound like progress. Funny though, she's not
tret any better. Kicked from pillar to post all her life.

She's not any of them things, as it happens.
She just don't like people.
She particularly don't like foreigners, which (*waves a hand*

over her face) she must've made an exception for at some time, though she's never explained why. Barely who.

Beat.

One of the walls of her heart is thicker than it should be.
Causes high blood pressure, hypertension, dizzy spells.
Collapses.
She's a proper case, not like most of these I deal with.
There's no way she can work. Fifty-eight years old, sick, thick, thinks a CV is an old French car, not getting a corner office is she?

The thing about ATOS is they're easy to play. They work on a target matrix, very much like us – this is the plus side of working for a payday loan company, it gives you a real insight into British society – and so you just play the matrix.
Play the spastic, basically. I know it sounds harsh but. . .

All you need to do, Mum, is be aware of *everything*.
All the innocent little things you do in everyday life, when you go in that office they are watching like a hawk and they *will* hold them against you.
Did you get up unaided?
Could you walk?
Then you're not physically impaired.

Did you respond straight away when they called your name?
Did you fill out the form by yourself?
You've not got mental problems.

They have hidden cameras in their offices so they can analyse all this at their leisure.

Well dressed is bad – awareness of social norms.
Pets are bad – ability to care for others.
Hobbies are bad – ability to function socially.

And all these abilities mean only one thing: *you can work*.

They take all the little things people do to make a good impression, the things we do to prove that we are human beings, and they use them to fuck you. That's the cruelty, the breathtaking cruelty of it.

To pass an ATOS assessment you have to be, or play, a locked-in idiot with no social skills, no friends, nobody that's ever loved them in the history of the world.
Boris Johnson, basically.

Mum's flapping, she's panicking, says she can't catch her breath. How'll she live without her money?
Stop flapping, I say.
It's them as don't know how the system works who need to worry.

Beat.

Summat odd came out of it, as it happens.
I was at a client's flat, she'd been tricky to get hold of, wriggles out of stuff, but finally I'd got hold of her, and Mum kept ringing. It were right embarrassing actually.

Now most of the kind I deal with would turn that to their advantage, but this lass . . .
'You alright?' she says.
Fine thanks. Let's get back to the matter at hand.
'Would you like a cup of tea?'

Don't like to be rude unless it's earned.

She sits me down at her kitchen table and we talk.
It's the expression on her face.

Carolina, her name is. Portuguese lass, on her own with a little kid. Jayden.
I don't like kids.
Think it's all about them, don't they?

We talk about this and that, but at the back of me mind I'm thinking 'What's your game? Are you trying to butter us up so I'll let you off your money?' Cos I can't do that.
But that face of hers.

Guileless, would be the word.
She just seemed to like us.

In the end she invited me round for tea. Tomorrow night.
She's making some Portuguese speciality with salt cod in it.
Sounds absolutely disgusting, to be honest, but . . .

I shouldn't really go. It's against policy and all that.
But I think she could do with the company.

Lights down on **Denise**. *Lights up on* **Stefano** *smoking furiously,*
pacing.

Stefano   Dead kids weigh fucking nothing.
That's what I've learned today.

You need a couple of men to haul an adult corpse out of the
water but it only takes one arm to haul in a dead kid. Course,
normally they've been in for a while, got waterlogged. This
lot were barely in half an hour. We hardly needed the boat,
could've waded out . . .

This morning, a migrant boat, unusually overloaded even by
the standards of migrant boats, overturned almost within
sight of Rabbit Beach. So far we're looking at north of 350
dead. Salvo and I personally recovered seventy-four corpses
today. Mainly children. Children and women. They run
women-only boats now, cos they weigh less and you can get
more in and then in the middle of the ocean, the smugglers
can stop the boat and say there's one more payment . . .

It's bad enough when they're aged twenty-five. When
they're five . . .

He stops pacing, squats, rubs his face with his hands for several
moments.

Last year the users of TripAdvisor voted Rabbit Beach the
most beautiful beach in the world. It's called Rabbit Beach
because we used to raise rabbits on it before the tourists
came. We're not a poetic people. Between tourism and the
immigrant game, supplying the refugee centre or working

for the NGOs, a lot of people on this island are making a lot of money all of a sudden.

God forbid anything stop the tourist industry.

The Russians are probably back there already, pleased to get it all to themselves apart from the odd corpse. Our lot rushing to serve them cold drinks.
They don't give a flying fuck about anyone, do they, the Russians?
'This is my holiday. I earned it.'
Ugly bastards too. When they sunbathe, the men look like the drowned but fatter.

The fucking *numbers*. We pulled out *four times* as many dead last year as the year before. FOUR TIMES. More than three thousand corpses. And those are just the ones we *found*.
This year, so far, **thirty** times as many.

But nothing changes. We're drowning in media, awash with politicians, but not a fucking thing changes. People keep pouring in, more boats than ever before, boats from Turkey and Lebanon and Libya and Egypt, boats with no crews that are set on a course to crash into Europe. Rescue guaranteed cos nobody wants a shipwreck off their coastline, so the price of the ticket goes up. Ingenious fuckers, the smugglers.

On the radio this morning, they said this is the biggest global mass migration since the Second World War. And all we do is let them drown.

I ask Sal what are we going to do.
'Drink,' he says, and marches off, big broad back to me, shoulders hunched up around his ears.

Beat.

Modibo is standing on the pier, staring at the rows of bodies, his face haunted. I can only guess what, *who*, he's thinking of. I realise I've never seen him without a smile before.
He turns to me and, very quietly, he says that it's deliberate.
That our glorious leaders *want* the migrants to drown, as a

deterrent, a warning to others. They want them to see TV footage of the bloated bodies and the rotted faces of those who trod the watery way of death before them, so they'll hesitate before they set foot in one of those rickety little deathtraps.

And he says they do see – and they get in anyway. They know what the dangers are, but they keep coming and coming because, in his words, 'if those men in their offices knew what we were coming from, they'd know we will never, ever stop.'

Pause.

We should have fucking done it. We should have . . . (*Beat.*) We got an alert. An hour before we went out. A civilian call: ship in distress. But you can't just take a boat out off your own bat, you have to get permission from the higher ups. So we called it in. And sat. And waited. And waited. And watched the hands of the clock tick by.

We could have saved them. Some of them. If we'd . . . Fuck me.

Beat.

It's not fucking fair. For them to be in sight of land, within touching distance of safety, and for the boat to go down, feels so fucking unfair. Maybe it's no worse than drowning in the middle of a blue desert and nobody knows you're gone, maybe there's no difference at the end of the day. I don't know.

All I can tell you is how I feel.

Lights down on **Stefano**. *Lights up on* **Denise**.

Denise   *Bacalau*, it's called.

The Portuguese salt cod thing. You have to soak it for 24 hours before you make it, which I were right touched by, that she'd gone to all that effort. Butter, potatoes, onions, garlic, peppers, parsley, then on top of that chopped olives and hard-boiled eggs!

She sticks a plateful in front of me and smiles, and I lift a forkful to me mouth and you know what I'm thinking . . . I'm from fucking *Leeds*, for fuck's sakes. This is not for me.

And it were delicious. It were absolutely delicious.

Two helpings and a bottle an' half of red later and we're gassing. Men, kids, jobs, family, the lot. She's not got a remarkable story, but it's not the remarkable stories that stick with you, is it?
Came over here to study English, met a fella, decided to stay, had Jayden, the fella fucked off. Why do men do that? It's like they live in a haze.
The thing about Carolina is she's not got an ounce of self-pity. She's right in the middle of telling me about her paediatric studies, I can't spell the word and she's studying it in a foreign language so fair play, and how the fees have gone way up and childcare is 'so fucking expensive in this country' – I love the way she says 'fucking' with that little growl, it's quite sexy actually – and so she's got behind with the rent and she's had to go to this arsehole company for money . . .

And we've both totally forgotten that's why I'm here.

And then she laughs, and I laugh, and she pours another glass of wine.

And so I tell her how to cancel the CPA we put on her account. Send a letter to her bank by registered post, five working days before payment is due, and we can't touch her. People are remarkably ignorant of their rights in this country.

Well. Least you can do when someone makes you dinner, ent it?

The touching thing is she's so bloody grateful. It's only a few months' breathing space but it seems to mean the world to her. Her fridge died last week. Jayden needs new shoes.

I don't make friends easily.
I'm not a giver. A confider. I cling on to what I am, my sense of self, like grim death, white bloody knuckles, because I've had to fight so bloody hard for every last inch of it.

But tonight I feel summat shift inside me.
And then the phone rings.

Lights down on **Denise**. *Lights up on* **Stefano**.

Stefano   I've not been able to sleep much.
Lot of nightmares.

The rotten fingers of the drowned clutching at my neck.
Grey faces of the long dead staring up from the seabed.
People I'd forgotten I'd fished out sitting on the end of the bed, glaring at me, seawater pooling on the sheets. They never speak, but the briny carrion stink of them . . .
Staring at me as if somehow I've betrayed them.

I swear I've woken up more than once because of the smell.
Open all the windows, turn the lights on. Nothing there, obviously.

Chiara understands but she doesn't understand, you know?
We have a deal. Don't bring the work home with you. Which is fair enough. And after a few nights she's starting to get pissed off. I've tried the sofa but the noise, well I don't believe I make any noise, but the kids come in frightened and Daddy's fine, he's fine, go back to bed . . .

Beat.

Difficult to speak to anyone. Salvo would use it to get at me, hide his own fears and worries. We're fishermen and fishermen die. You're not supposed to make a big deal of death, you mourn and you get back to life while you've still got it. But there's never been a time when three hundred and fifty have died at once. In sight of shore. With no-one to mourn for them.

Which is why the only one who understands is Modibo.

He doesn't ask me about it, he just listens. He understands, not the words sometimes but the gist. They've all *seen* it, been through it, know people who've not survived.
They know what's really happening.

He's got temporary leave to remain.
I guess his story checks out, though God knows how they make these decisions anyway. The light of joy in his face when he found out. The pure, unadulterated joy. Jumping and hugging with his mates and the happiness on their faces too, when half of them won't get what he's got and'll get sent back and they all know that, but they were really genuinely happy for him. Fucking lifts your heart.

It's been bloody good for me to be around him, actually.
He's been a real mate.

So I'm going to be a good mate back.

Lights down on **Stefano**. *Lights up on* **Denise**.

Denise   I try not to go. I tell Caroline it's just me mum, this is what she's like. Attention-seeking. It won't be serious. Bit of asthma. But she insists. 'It's your mother. Of course I'll drive you.'

I hate going over there. The state of the place.
The grime between the bathroom tiles.
The ring of encrusted shit around the toilet.
The memories of boredom and terror.

In the whole flat there's not a single book. How is that even possible? Not a book, not a picture, not a piece of culture in the whole house, never has been. Nothing to connect her to the rest of the human race. No food in the fridge. And it'd be fine if Mum were happy with that, but she hates it. All she ever does is moan.

It scares the shit out of me. It fucking terrifies me that I could end up like that, like a dried fly the spider forgot to eat. It's what keeps me going, keeps me pressing . . .

There's no reason for me to feel guilty. She doesn't like me, never has. But I go in and I see *my* mum lying on't floor, gasping for air, in the midst of all this squalor, and nobody gives a toss and I'm the one that's supposed to. And then Carolina steps through the door, and the look she gives me when she sees the state Mum's living in . . .

A *flood* of shame. I see the mildewed curtains and peeling ceilings in a whole new light then.

Paramedics are very quick. They said it were probably down to stress on top of her existing condition. Does she have anything in particular worrying her? Anything that might have stressed her out at all?

Beat.

It's a heart attack.

Lights down on **Denise**. *Lights up on* **Stefano**.

Stefano   He's sent for Aminata.
His wife.
He says if he's going to be here that long, he can't stand to be without her.
Which means she's got to come in by the same route.

Beat.

Aminata's boat left Libya yesterday morning. It's a thirty-six-hour journey on average, depending on the engine and if the boat's only overloaded or fucking overloaded. But if the weather's rough, and the forecast is brutal, it can take days.

The most terrifying bit for the families of migrants, and I'd never even thought about this, is that when they undertake the crossing itself they're completely out of contact. The rest of the way they've got phones, they can keep in touch, but when they enter the Blue Desert they disappear. Sitting there, staring at your phone, wondering if the person you love is ever going to ring it again.

Days of staring at his phone. Wondering if she's ever going to ring again.

I'm going to take the boat out tonight and try to find her. (*Beat.*) Least I can do.

Beat.

The look on Modibo's face when I tell him.
He gives me a photo of her and tells me to take care. To come back safe.
Both of us.

Lights down on **Stefano**. *Lights up on* **Denise**.

Denise   They turf Mum out of hospital a few days later. The nurses, who are *lovely*, want to keep her in another week, but the consultant, who's a shiny-haired *cunt*, mutters 'bed blockers' and saunters off. I shout after him, 'Are bed blockers not the same as sick people?', but he doesn't stop, urgent golf course to attend to. So out she goes.

Pitiful state, can barely hobble to the bus stop. Naturally she doesn't want my help, snaps at me if I try to hold her arm. I watch her stagger and wheeze through the puddles in the car park, almost on hands and knees, and I think, 'Come on then ATOS, have a look at this and call her 'fit for work'.

I don't even coach her for the interview. Piece of piss. 'You just go in there, Mum, and be your natural warm and vibrant self, and we will be just fine.'

Watch her dress in the same old shabby shit she's been wearing for donkey's years, take a full ninety-two seconds to hobble from waiting room to office, drool slightly onto her forms, and I'm thinking: we've got no problem here. And when the bastard shifts slightly in his seat and starts throwing the odd question my way, not many, no alarm bells go off. I know how to handle them.

Beat.

I 'provide her with sufficient support structure to facilitate a return to paid employment.' Without me she'd get the 15 points you need for Employment Support Allowance, but given my 'obvious capacity to compensate for the applicant's own shortcomings . . .'

This woman I've spent my whole life trying to get away from, they're tethering me to her. Til the day she dies.

I go mad. Three days solid on the phone arguing she meets Exceptional Circumstances under Regulation 25, she's limited capacity for work-related activity, Regulation 31.

They *hate* that. They blank me and block me and fob me off, tens of thousands of pounds in man hours to deny us this pitifully, embarrassingly small sum of money, and I keep pushing and pushing, and I hear the vitriol in their voices.

But I win. I fight and scratch and play them at their own game til in the end they refer the case to an appeals tribunal. The set-up there is still rigged, but they've gotta be a bit more public about it, which gives you a chance.

I prepare meticulously.
Go through all the documentation.
Get Mum ready. No stone unturned this time.
Go over me speech time after time.

The tribunal is this Thursday.

Lights down on **Denise***. Lights up on* **Stefano** *soaking wet, totally drenched.*

Stefano   It's still at first, but right from the off you can tell it's coming. Salvo muttering and staring up at the sky. In the dark we can't see the black clouds building up, but we can feel them. Sticky. Static.

Then the wind picks up, and the waves start to lift the boat and dump it back down again. You can tell how much trouble you're in at sea by how hard the boat thumps down between swells, and we're hitting the water harder and harder. Water is rock hard when you hit it like that. Your fillings jar in your mouth. Rain thrashes on the windscreen. Something shatters on the console.

The pauses at the top of the swells get longer and longer, huge waves loom out of the dark like sea monsters, and then the sickening lurch down into the trough and the THUMP vibrating through your guts and bones. Sal is screaming at me, screaming at the top of his lungs and I can still barely hear him, that this is insane and he's turning us back when suddenly, not far away, in between giant swells, I spot a light. Low in the water, pitching and yawing, obviously in big trouble.

A migrant boat.

I scream at Sal to head towards it and he doesn't want to, you can see he's afraid for us but what kind of coastguard, what kind of man, leaves a boat to go down? We swing around, which means we're perpendicular to the waves, they're crashing across us, drenching us, and that is when you can go under. I'm raging at Sal, veins popping, throat raw, to get us back in line, get us back in line, when there's a flash of lightning and out of the corner of my eye, this Leviathan looms. A monstrous wave as tall as a tower block, so tall it has little waterfalls tumbling from its crest.

I freeze. And Sal freezes. And Leviathan pounces.

A roar, and it slams us under its paw, and the whole boat goes under. The monster presses us down down down into the depths, and I breathe salt water and I don't know whether to cling onto the boat or let it sink and take my chances, and I realise it doesn't matter.
It doesn't matter what I do.

Beat.

And then, for some reason, for no *reason*, the boat squirms free and we pop out onto the surface, gasping and choking, the roar of the storm louder than ever. I look at Sal and he's pale as death, pale as one of the drowned. We're heading into the teeth of the storm, every time we climb one of the waves I don't think we're gonna reach the top, but we do and we're getting there. We're getting closer and closer to the light, maybe a couple of hundred metres at most. And then, all of a sudden, it goes out. The light vanishes.

Sal hunches over the wheel and his knuckles whiten even more and he kicks out at the boat, screaming at it, pick the fuck up you fuck, you fuck, you fucker, but all that picks up is the wind. The storm holds us at arm's length, watching us squirm and strive, laughing at us, refusing to let us get any closer. For half an hour we make no headway.

And then all of a sudden the wind drops. And the noises start.

Beat.

A loud thump against the hull.
A pause.
And then another thump, and then another, and another.

Most of the equipment is broken or gone but one of the terawatt lights is still intact, and I don't want to turn it on, please don't make me turn it on, but I turn it on and in the conical glare of light we see them coming, the storm mockingly pushing them towards us.

The black silhouettes of corpses.

Dozens of corpses are floating in the water around us. Thumps against the hull coming in twos and threes. I grab the first body I can, wrench it halfway aboard, turn it over, and . . .

It's got Modibo's face.

I don't mean the body *looks* like Modibo, he *is* Modibo. He's got my friend's face, but dead and gone.

I scream in pure terror and drop the body back in the ocean. Sal staring at me like I've lost my mind. I lean back against the side and howl like a child. Sal shakes me, slaps me across the face. 'You fucking brought us out here. You do your fucking job. Get them in.' I pull myself up, lean over the side, drag another one in, flip him over, and..

He's got Modibo's face.
Every one of the fifty-seven bodies I recovered that night had Modibo's face.

But I keep pulling them in. If I can't bring her back alive, at least I can bring her back.

Lights down on **Stefano**. *Lights up on* **Denise**, *holding a small urn.*

Denise   Mum died the night before the tribunal. Massive coronary. Instantaneous.

There'll be an inquest but the paramedic, same fella as the time before, very kind, he said it's almost impossible to tell. If the worry killed her, or it would've happened anyway with her condition.

But I know.

Beat.

There were three people at the funeral.
The priest.
The fella who presses the button to send the stiff down into the fiery furnace. Who was chewing gum and staring out the window the entire time. Commitment to excellence.
And me.

And then it were five.
Carolina and Jayden turned up. Poor little bugger. Top day out for him.

I couldn't cry at first. You feel obliged to cry. But I couldn't. Til she turned up.
Tears from kindness. Just leaked out. Why are people kind? It's the most unlikely thing.

(*Indicates urn.*) Think I'll take her ashes up the moors on a windy day. Mum hated walking, absolutely loathed it. Exactly where she wouldn't want to be.

Scatter them far and wide. As far away as possible.
Bye Mum.

Been telling meself that for a while now.
Still got 'em, though. For some reason.
I've wanted to be unyoked from you for so long, and now it's happened I . . .

Beat.

I go back to work straight after the funeral. Uni won't let me graduate if I don't pay the fees. Cuts are biting, loans are rising. Plenty of work. They say it's a 'recovery' but it's not a fucking recovery in Beeston, let me tell you that.

But suddenly all their flats look like Mum's.
The same streaks of filth on the walls. The same worn-through carpet with the underlay showing. The same sense of hopelessness and helplessness.

And then the other day summat proper mad happens.
I'm collecting off this old lady and she's in floods, which is obviously hard but after a while you get a bit hardened to it, you think maybe they're turning the waterworks on for your benefit, though this one seemed genuine enough.
Eventually she stops crying and turns to reach into her handbag, and when she turns back, she has Mum's face.
Her dead grey stare, full of reproach.

Fucking hell.

I gave the old dear another week and sprint out the door, down the stairs, can't wait for the lift, flight after flight of stairs, she lives on the fourteenth floor, and behind me her tearful voice echoing down the stairwell, calling out in gratitude.

I quit me job that afternoon.
Packed it in. I just fucking couldn't do it any more,
you know?

Lights down on **Denise**. *Lights up on* **Stefano**.

Stefano   We found her.

It took all night but we found her.

There were only three people pulled alive out of the sea that
night, and Aminata was one of them.

We travel back in the breaking dawn. Grey turning orange
turning blue. Five live bodies and fifty-seven dead ones.
Nobody says a word, each ocean-deep in their own thoughts.
Sal kicks me and nods at Aminata and says, 'Is it her? Is that
why we came?' And I nod.

'I have a son,' is all he says to me. 'A *son*.'
No more words til we reach land.

We pull up to the pier. It's packed, a wall of people, and I'm
scanning for Modibo's face but there's a splash, Aminata's
over the side and into the shallows and there's a kind of
keening noise from the pier and a second splash and it's
him, he's in the water too! These two torpedoes rocketing
together to meet in an explosion of sheer joy and relief.
Limbs entangled, rolling over, yelling, laughing, water
splashing everywhere, this fantastical new sea creature.
Tears and hands over mouths and hugging on the pier.
Even Salvo's got tears in his eyes, the old cynic, though
he's trying to hide them. I tell him thanks. He turns away,
but he hears me.

I have never seen two happier people in all my born days.

Me? I still have fifty-seven bodies to unload.

Lights down on **Stefano**. *Lights up on* **Denise**.

Denise   I can't go out for a couple of days. Even though it's
final lectures and I am *so far* behind.

A knock on my locked door.
'You're not answering your phone.'
Carolina?
Yeah, no, I'm fine.
I think she's gone away. And then she says,
'Listen, you might think it's crazy, but will you move in with us?'
What? What you talking about?
'The couch folds out. If we split the rent I can start to pay my loan.'
Is this a joke?
'I trust you,' she says.
'I don't trust easily but I trust you. I don't know why.
Will you think about it?
Please?'

Beat.

Fucking hell. Fucking, fucking hell.
Why are people kind?

I just received this. Delivered this morning.
Exam results.

The last question on me last exam was on the monkey trap. You know the one. Where the monkey can get its hand into the coconut shell to pull out treats but it can't pull out its fist with the treats in them, so the villagers can catch it. The question was, 'What does this experiment suggest about the perils of untrammelled materialism?'

You could see the answer they wanted. This home of original thinking.

But the monkey trap's always meant summat different to me.
Cos I've never had the balls to put in me hand in in't first place.
Never could admit there was anything I wanted, because I knew I couldn't have it and I'd only get hurt.

So I took a different tack.
I wrote that empirical studies of the monkey trap
experiment do not support the presumed hypothesis of
inherent greed. To wit: in the vast majority of test cases, the
monkeys let go of the treats. They demonstrate a clear
understanding of the relative importance of grated coconut
vis-à-vis their own bollocks.

That's not me answer word for word, obviously.
I wrote that the monkey trap experiment is fundamentally
an indicator of *hope*. It speaks to our ability to walk away
from delusions, from traps. To save ourselves from our baser
instincts.

Me last line, and I can't believe I actually wrote this hippy
shit but fuck it, was, 'Perhaps the ultimate purpose of the
experiment is for the monkeys to teach us something.'

Lights stay up on **Denise**. *She kneels to the urn. Lights come up on*
Stefano.

Stefano   They had their second wedding today.
Their 'European wedding', they called it. To celebrate her
coming back from the dead.
Chiara loaned her a dress, looked really good on her
actually.

Nothing fancy, just a party in the camp.
Malian food and music.
Dancing and laughing and hugging and more dancing. I'm
completely shattered.
Dragged Sal along, after much protest. He's still dancing.
Didn't think much of the food though.

I was the guest of honour. Imagine that. The bloody guest of
honour.

They've given us joy.
And hope.
They've brought us the things we have nothing of.
And I thank them for that.

They don't know what'll happen. If either of them will get to stay long-term. But they're here, in this moment, alive and living. And that is all you can ask for.

I defy you to see the joy in Modibo and Aminata's faces and not feel hope.
I defy you.

Stefano *and* **Denise** *look warily at one another.*
Denise *empties the ashes.*

'Lampedusa' starts to play.

Blackout.

End of play.

Performance Rights

Bloomsbury Methuen Drama Contemporary Dramatists

include

John Arden (two volumes)
Arden & D'Arcy
Peter Barnes (three volumes)
Sebastian Barry
Mike Bartlett
Dermot Bolger
Edward Bond (eight volumes)
Howard Brenton (two volumes)
Leo Butler
Richard Cameron
Jim Cartwright
Caryl Churchill (two volumes)
Complicite
Sarah Daniels (two volumes)
Nick Darke
David Edgar (three volumes)
David Eldridge (two volumes)
Ben Elton
Per Olov Enquist
Dario Fo (two volumes)
Michael Frayn (four volumes)
John Godber (four volumes)
Paul Godfrey
James Graham
David Greig
John Guare
Lee Hall (two volumes)
Katori Hall
Peter Handke
Jonathan Harvey (two volumes)
Iain Heggie
Israel Horovitz
Declan Hughes
Terry Johnson (three volumes)
Sarah Kane
Barrie Keeffe
Bernard-Marie Koltès (two volumes)
Franz Xaver Kroetz
Kwame Kwei-Armah
David Lan
Bryony Lavery
Deborah Levy
Doug Lucie

David Mamet (four volumes)
Patrick Marber
Martin McDonagh
Duncan McLean
David Mercer (two volumes)
Anthony Minghella (two volumes)
Tom Murphy (six volumes)
Phyllis Nagy
Anthony Neilson (two volumes)
Peter Nichol (two volumes)
Philip Osment
Gary Owen
Louise Page
Stewart Parker (two volumes)
Joe Penhall (two volumes)
Stephen Poliakoff (three volumes)
David Rabe (two volumes)
Mark Ravenhill (three volumes)
Christina Reid
Philip Ridley (two volumes)
Willy Russell
Eric-Emmanuel Schmitt
Ntozake Shange
Sam Shepard (two volumes)
Martin Sherman (two volumes)
Christopher Shinn
Joshua Sobel
Wole Soyinka (two volumes)
Simon Stephens (three volumes)
Shelagh Stephenson
David Storey (three volumes)
C. P. Taylor
Sue Townsend
Judy Upton
Michel Vinaver (two volumes)
Arnold Wesker (two volumes)
Peter Whelan
Michael Wilcox
Roy Williams (four volumes)
David Williamson
Snoo Wilson (two volumes)
David Wood (two volumes)
Victoria Wood

For a complete listing of Bloomsbury
Methuen Drama titles, visit:

www.bloomsbury.com/drama

Follow us on Twitter and keep up to date
with our news and publications

@MethuenDrama